Impersonations

From boyhood to manhood. Iron sharpens iron.

Jonathan Oliver

" J.O. "

HIGHER ENLIGHTENMENT

ISBN: 978-0-9969487-0-8
PUBLISHED BY HIGHER
ENLIGHTENMENT
www.higherenlightenment.com

Printed in the United States of America

This book is dedicated to my mom and dad. You loved me in the best way you knew...imperfectly perfect. I wouldn't be the person I am today if it wasn't for your prayers, support and love. Thank you.

Acknowledgments

I am so blessed to be surrounded by people who believe in me. These people have believed in my dreams, my potential, my plans, and my goals. Fortunately for me, at those times when it was hard for me to believe in myself, their collective belief held me up and kept me going

For believing it was possible for me to write this book and that I had the ability to follow it through to completion, I thank my best friend and closest love, Saran George. I acknowledge Michael Taylor, my mentor, for encouraging me to stretch and become a more authentic man. I am grateful to my book coach, Cassandra Skogmo. God placed you in my life at the perfect time, Cass. Thank you for being so patient and understanding as we made this journey together. I am thankful to DaRhonda Williams for lighting a fire under my butt and encouraging me to write Impersonations in the first place. I am indebted to my graphic designer, Kris Jones, for designing an amazing book cover.

I am honored by the love and support of my mother, Kathleen Martin, and her husband and my stepdad, Bobby C. Martin; my father Dywarne Terry Oliver, Sr., and his wife and my step mom, L. C. Oliver; my brothers, Dywarne Oliver and Bobby E. Martin; my great-grandmother, Nettie Wilson; and my grandmothers, Mila Wade and Ellen Fillmore. I bless my pastors for setting a loving example and for always being approachable as I traveled through different stages in my life: Pastor Fred Jones, Pastor Leslie Chandler Jr., Pastor Bobby King, Sr., Pastor L. D.

Thomlinson, Pastor G. T. Curry, Sr., and Pastor Bryan Carter. I extend special thanks to the ManKind Project of Houston and the ManKind Project of North Texas for helping me see myself more clearly as a complete man and to the Kingsmen-I-Group for helping me see that I am imperfectly perfect. And to Ken Nieser and Jim Temple, thank you for helping me keep my sanity during this entire process. Finally, with deep gratitude for my entire family, my friends, and everyone else who has impacted my writing…this is my gift to you.

Foreword
by Michael Taylor

Every now and then a book comes along that has the power to shift the consciousness of an entire group of people. Jonathan Oliver's book, *Impersonations*, is that book. This book is a must-read for any man who is courageous enough to begin or continue his personal journey of self-discovery. It should become a handbook that men keep in their pockets to refer to when they are asking the question, "What does it really mean to be a man?"

With the wisdom of a man far surpassing his years, Jonathan writes about the struggles and victories of becoming a man. In clear concise words coupled with deeply felt emotion, he guides the reader on a quest for authenticity. His story helps guide readers to insights about themselves that will surely empower them to remove the culturally generated masks that most men hide behind today.

The time has come for men to create a new paradigm of masculinity and this book will definitely become a beacon for men who choose to embrace its message. It is a book whose time has come and a message of hope for men of all ethnicities and social backgrounds. The underlying message of the book is for men to stop pretending and to become authentically empowered to be who they really are. The world needs to hear this message and Jonathan Oliver is the perfect man to deliver it.

Michael Taylor is a student and teacher of life who has a passion for empowering others to reach their full potential. When he's not writing or speaking, you will find him spending time in nature or simply hanging out with his wife, Bedra.

A Note to the Reader

Impersonations is the story of my life, so far, and in it I share my mission and my shadows. My shadows are the parts of myself that I repress and hide from people—the tug-of-war between my mind, feelings, body and spirit. My shadows create a world of self-doubt through lying, controlling and manipulation. My mission is to create a world of truth, love and faith by motivating and educating people, basing my work on the message of Jesus Christ. What a relief it has been to discover gold, not only in my mission but in my shadows. I couldn't have written this book without going through the pain of self-discovery and healing, and I have dug deep into my shadows and in that learning process, polished the gold I found there. I have stayed the course in doing my mission with the help of my affirmation: As a man among men I am faithful and true. And I have been inspired by the words of Robert Bly: "We know that shame often keeps us from meeting other peoples' eyes—or our own. But when we do look into our own eyes, whether we do that staring into a mirror, or into a pond surface—we have the inescapable impression, so powerful and astonishing, that someone is looking back at us."

My purpose in writing *Impersonations* is to draw the members of my family closer to one another. It is my hope that my entire family—from the roots of the family tree to the tips of its branches—can find the way to live as one working unit. I want us to eliminate any envy we have of one another, replacing it with supportive behaviors. Not just support for some of us—those who seem to be making good choices or the choices we want them to make—but support for each member of our family. I want us to stop quietly stabbing each other in the back and begin loving one another unconditionally, without judgment. I want us to celebrate our unique differences in a manner that will allow us to serve a cause greater than ourselves. In particular, I want each man in my family to look into the eyes of the man in the mirror, search his soul and begin living with greater integrity, accountability and authenticity. And as I look back at what I have written, it is clear to me that the condition of my family is also the condition of the larger family of man, of people everywhere, and I know that the larger condition can only improve if we, my family and I, find healthy ways to improve.

In 2007 I attended a philanthropy summit in Dallas, Texas, where I had the opportunity to hear W. Wilson Goode speak. Mr. Goode is a former mayor of Philadelphia, Pennsylvania, and founder of Amachi, the nationally acclaimed, unique partnership of secular and faith-based organizations working together to provide mentoring to children of incarcerated parents. "Amachi" is a Nigerian Ibo word that means "Who knows what God has brought us through this child." Mr. Goode shared a revealing truth through the telling of the following story.

A little boy was outside playing one day when he decided he wanted to play ball with his dad, so he ran inside calling, "Daddy, Daddy, let's go play catch." The father was watching a football game and he said, "Son, my team is on the goal line and they are about to score. Come back in five minutes." Like persistent little children do, the little boy returned in five minutes. And he said again, "Daddy, Daddy, let's go play catch." The father replied, "Son, the other team is driving down the field with the ball and I want to see if they are going to score or not. Come back in five more minutes." Like a good little boy, the child agreed, "OK,

Dad." Five minutes later the little boy came back and said, "Daddy, Daddy, let's go play catch!" By this time the father knew that he didn't really want to play catch. So he took a map of the world and tore it into a bunch of pieces and said to his son, "When you put this map back together, we will go play catch." The little boy gathered up all the pieces of the map and ran outside. Three minutes later the little boy ran back in and shouted, "Daddy, Daddy, I put the map back together! Now can we go play catch?" The father replied, "Hold on, how did you put that map of the world back together so quickly?" The little boy said, "Daddy, on the back of the map was a picture of a man. When I put the pieces of the man together, I put the world back together."

So, I pray that the blessings I have received by writing *Impersonations* will flow over and into my family and on down to other people in my life—to my friends and their families—supporting and encouraging them all to share their gifts and spread their love and, by doing so, put the pieces of themselves back together.

And finally, I humbly gift this book to the world with a huge, heartfelt hope that it helps put the world back together, one man at a time.

In joy,

Jonathan Oliver

Impersonations

I gaze out of my window at a gorgeous afternoon. There are bright, puffy, white clouds in the sky. There is a breeze barely blowing through the tree tops. Spring is almost over and that Texas summer heat is fast approaching. As I let this moment settle over me, I am at the greatest place in my life.

I have an amazing girlfriend who I have been dating for nearly three years, and we are preparing to take premarital classes this fall. She is as magnificent on the inside as she is gorgeous on the outside. My mom and stepdad are in good health. Their relationship is as strong as it has ever been and my stepdad and I are closer than ever before. My dad and I have a father-son relationship that lifts my heart to the heavens in joy. We are friends and talk together now about real-life situations and our conversations only grow us closer. My older brother recently got married and he seems to be getting his life in order and I am thankful. My little brother is doing great and is becoming a better man each passing day. My paternal great-grandmother is eighty-eight years old, in good health and still able to take care of herself. My maternal grandmother is eighty-seven and even though she lives in a nursing home, bound to a bed, her mind is still very sharp and witty. My grandmother who lives in Houston is one of my closest friends and her advice is always spot on. I am at the greatest place in my life.

My own motivational company, Higher Enlightenment, is beginning to grow. Its mission is to create a world of truth, love, and faith by motivating and educating people, and spreading the word of Jesus Christ. During my first year, I scheduled one speaking engagement at a high school where a buddy of mine coaches for a Fellowship of Christian Athletes' program. The next year I joined Toastmasters and, as a result, I scheduled fifteen speaking engagements. Now, in just the first quarter of 2008, my third year, I have had over forty speaking engagements. I am an independent contractor with a company that sends me all over the country to speak with high school juniors about how to find the right college and with high school seniors about how to make their college education and career count. I am at the greatest place in my life.

As I take in a deep breath and exhale, I give thanks that I am in the best shape physically since I played collegiate football. I have dozens of great, genuine friendships. My high school class reunion is next month—I can't wait to catch up with all of my old friends. I have an awesome part-time job at a restaurant which feels more like fun with my family than actual work at what happens to be the number one steakhouse in Texas. As summer approaches, I have even managed to shoot a few pars on a nearby golf course; not many, but a few.

At this very moment I am sober. My recovery program isn't perfect nor does it have to be. I am learning every day that it's "progress, not perfection" and, like a buddy of mine who is also in recovery once told me, "I am right where I am supposed to be." However, what is most important at this very moment is that I am authentic, sincere, accountable, and in integrity.

As I continue to gaze out my window on this beautiful afternoon, I know that my life has not always been like it is today and who's to say that tomorrow won't bring rain. But right now it is what it is and as my mind begins to drift back through my past, I am reminded that success is not a destination, but a journey, and as I reflect on my own journey, I know that the Lord has brought me a mighty long way....

Chapter 1
Making Fun to Hide the Truth

"Therefore Sarah laughed to herself…And the Lord asked Abraham, Why did Sarah laugh…Then Sarah denied it, saying, I did not laugh; for she was afraid. And He said, No, but you did laugh." -Genesis 18:12-15 (AMP)

When I was in elementary school, around the fifth grade, I had a girlfriend. For a reason I have since forgotten, I decided to end our relationship and I thought the kindest way to do it was to tell her the truth about how I felt in a letter. So I did, and I gave the letter to her the next day during recess. She sent me a reply, but she also took things a step further. Her reply included the letter I had originally written, with every misspelled word circled and every grammar mistake underlined in bright red ink! I was so embarrassed, but she didn't stop there. She showed the letter to all of her girlfriends and to all of my buddies. Everyone laughed—they all thought it was so funny. I laughed too, and I made up whatever excuse I could think of at the time to make it seem like it was no big deal.

The truth? It *was* a big deal, and deep down within myself, I wasn't laughing at all. I felt like an absolute idiot. Hiding the truth hurt.

Unintentionally mispronouncing words, writing words incorrectly, using a word in the wrong context, or mixing up phrases—no matter the situation, the results were always the same—laughter, laughter, and more laughter, and me laughing, too, because what else can you do when everyone in the classroom, in the hallway and out on the playground is laughing at you. When all of your friends are pointing their fingers and holding their stomachs while laughing at you, what can you do but make fun of yourself and laugh with them. But, again, inside, it was no laughing matter.

I began to wonder and ask myself why I did things the way I did. Why did I write that? Why did I think that? Why did that word sound the way it did in my head, but not show up on paper the way I thought it would when I wrote it. The truth—I was a pretty sharp kid. I didn't have a problem speaking in class, or anywhere else, for that matter, and I made friends very easily. More truth— I was always afraid of getting busted like I did when I wrote that break-up letter to my old girlfriend.

I never felt so weak and exposed to the world as I did when I had to write essays during class or take a spelling test without a word bank. The most terrifying times of all were when I had to read aloud in class. I remember how I would count from the person who read first and then, according to the direction in which we were going, I would figure out which paragraph I was going to have to read when it was my turn. I would read that paragraph over and over to myself. If I had trouble sounding out a word, I would ask the kid sitting behind me if he knew the word. Right before my turn, I would get this warm sensation on the back of my neck and upon finishing, I would feel shame. Even if I didn't sound stupid, I felt dumb in my head. If luck was with me and I didn't get called on to read during class that day, I felt like I had dodged a bullet.

After my experience with my ex-girlfriend (the copy editor from hell), I knew I was going to have to come up with something soon if I was going to enjoy my remaining school years and not be known as the "slow kid." Actually, the truth was, when it came to schoolwork, I was the kid who once I worked hard enough to really wrap my mind around a concept, I could move on and excel in that area, especially if it gave me the opportunity to openly express myself.

My third grade teacher, Mrs. Dodge, loved to make learning fun. In her class we were expected to think quick on our feet— responding to addition and subtraction problems not only accurately but quickly. So, for practice, every Friday Mrs. Dodge would let us play a math game called "around the world" and even though I didn't like math, I loved playing that game. The rules of the game were simple. One kid would stand beside another who remained seated at his desk. Then Mrs. Dodge would show the two of them a flash card, for example, 16 + 4. Whoever shouted out the correct answer first got to reach into the grab bag for a treat—a piece of candy, a toy or a pencil. If the kid who was sitting shouted "twenty!" first, besides getting a treat, he would stand up and move on "around the world" to stand beside another seated student, and the kid who had been standing would have to sit down in the "winner's" desk. Every night at home I would practice my addition and subtraction facts because I loved seeing how far around the world I could get. Those Friday games of "around the world" were the only times I truly enjoyed math.

Starting in fourth grade and then on through middle school, I was sent to a special education class. It was only for thirty minutes a day and just for the first few weeks of September. At first, I didn't know it was a special education class. But I figured it out one day while I watched my buddies make fun of other students who attended the class with me. The last thing I needed was my friends knowing I was in a class with those kids, so, again, there I was in a situation where I felt I had to hide the truth. I was getting pretty good at it, and so it wasn't too difficult for me to come up with a valid reason for why I missed thirty minutes of my regular class every day.

Also, at first, I didn't know why I was scheduled to attend those special classes. I knew I was doing well enough to remain in a regular classroom, but I figured maybe my teachers wanted me to get some extra help at the beginning of the year because they knew I struggled initially with certain materials. I discovered later, it was because of my scores on the TAAS tests.

In third grade I took the first of a series of tests which back then were called the Texas Assessment of Academic Skills (TAAS). Now they're called the Texas Assessment of Knowledge and Skills (TAKS). The purpose of the TAAS tests was to test students' abilities in the areas of reading, writing, and math. From the perspective of a third grader's mind, I didn't think the test was all that important. I would get my test scores back and look over them and even though I didn't do too well, I felt it was OK because I wasn't going to have to take the test again for another couple of years, and as all third graders know, two years is a long time!

It was at some point in middle school that I finally caught on to what was happening. My TAAS scores and my grades were completely at odds. I had continued to do poorly on the TAAS tests but I also continued to bring home fairly good grades on my report card. One day it just dawned on me. No wonder I was spending the first couple of weeks of each year in special education. I was bombing the TAAS exam and my teachers knew I needed some extra help. It felt really good to know that my teachers believed in me and had faith in my abilities. They didn't give up on me. They sent me to the special education classes where they knew I would catch up quickly with the one-on-one lessons those classes could provide. From that point on I became inspired and determined to do well in school even though it meant I would have to spend more time (well, maybe a lot more time) studying.

In eighth grade my determination began to pay off. We were assigned a research project that weighed heavily on whether we passed or failed. We had to select a topic, use several sources, write the paper, and cite my sources correctly in a bibliography. We had something like a month and a half to finish the assignment. In between my other classes and playing sports, I worked my butt off on that project. I wanted to prove to myself that I was capable of not just getting it done, but of doing a great job. I needed more time than most of the other kids to piece my project together, so I got permission from my teachers to skip out on recess and sometimes I was able to leave lunch early. When the time came to turn in my project, I felt I had given it my best. A few weeks later, my entire eighth grade class met in the library and the teachers gave out awards to students who did exceptionally well on their projects. Now, to be honest with you, I don't remember what my research project was about or what my grade was. What I do remember is that I was given the "Above and Beyond" award for my hard work and determination. I did prove to myself that I was capable of achieving a good grade if I worked a little harder, and that was a great feeling, but to be recognized by my teachers in front of my peers was priceless.

That same year I was asked by my English teacher, Mrs. Lawson, to be in the school play. I jumped at the chance. Here was another opportunity to push myself to be my best. The play was Thornton Wilder's classic, *Our Town*. Set at the turn of the 20th century, the play reveals the ordinary lives of people living in the small town of Grover's Corners, New Hampshire. The play focuses first on the routines and tiny necessities of daily life, and then delves into deeper themes of love, marriage and death. I played a character named George. I studied that play until I knew not only my lines, but everyone else's, too. I didn't really memorize my lines—I became them. I became George. Bruce Lee once said, "If you try to memorize, then you will lose. Empty your mind and become like water. Now if you put water in a glass it will become the glass. If you put water in a teapot it will become the teapot. Water can flow, creep, drip, and crash. Water can become any shape it desires. Empty your mind and become like water." For years after the play ended, I could still remember some of those lines.

I always knew that I was a smart kid and so by the time I reached high school and looked back at the challenges of my elementary and middle school years—in spite of the taunting and joking, the time spent in special ed classes, and the extra time and effort I had to put into studying—things seemed to be going along pretty well. That is until I was told something that really got my attention: if I didn't pass the TAAS tests, I wouldn't participate in my senior year graduation ceremonies.

My older brother had already experienced this. He had not passed the math section of the TAAS in time to graduate with his class. Dywarne is four years older than me, and my baby brother and I always expected him to be the first of us three to walk across the stage and get his diploma. I remember Mom picking me up from school and telling me and my little brother that Dywarne wouldn't be graduating. I had felt so much shame for him, and I feared what could happen if I didn't begin to do better on the TAAS tests.

Somehow, my grandparents on my dad's side of the family never got the news that Dywarne wasn't graduating. I guess it was assumed that he would inform the people who were expecting to see him graduate. What I feel is that Dywarne thought that it would all just take care of itself…it didn't. Our grandparents drove four hours from Abilene, Texas, to attend the graduation ceremonies and after sitting in the bleachers watching everyone whose last name started with the letter O walk by, they realized something was wrong. Then they had to walk down from the bleachers and out of the stadium while everyone around them celebrated. I remember feeling embarrassment for my family and my older brother. He could have been knocked down for good. However, he got back up and passed the TAAS test later that summer with the help of our grandmother. What mattered the most was that he graduated. He will always be honored as the first in our family to have done that.

Nevertheless, I still needed to pass the TAAS for me and my dreams. That exam kept invading my life like a monster in a bad nightmare; whenever I thought it was over and done with, it would reappear. I came to the conclusion the only way to conquer the TAAS test was to face it head on. Hoping that somehow I would slip through the cracks and get a free pass card or that I would just study and, with a little luck, barely pass, were not options. I had no other choice but to look that TAAS test monster straight in the eye and give it all I had. As I reflected on the opportunity I had before me, I remembered what my Big Mama used to tell me about forming a relationship with God: you can't go over Him because He is too high, you can't go under Him because He is too low, and can't go around Him because He is too wide, so you must go through Him.

Sister Chandler, our pastor's wife, was a geometry teacher at the Giddings State School, a correctional institute for juveniles. Sister Chandler was able to access old TAAS exams. She agreed to tutor me and so every day after football practice, my mom would drive me out to the Chandlers' farm near the edge of town where we would maneuver around their very protective dogs and

Mom would leave me there to study with Sister Chandler for two or three hours and then return to pick me up. Over the course of my freshman year and before the last semester of my senior year, I took the writing section of the TAAS test twice, the reading section twice, and the math section six times. I passed the reading and writing sections by the end of my sophomore year, but there I was, a senior and still struggling with the math. I felt like the end was so close, yet so far away. Thank God for Sister Chandler who continued to tutor me and to encourage me not to give up. Pastor Chandler taught trigonometry at the Giddings State School and he made time to work with me and motivate me also. One of the most difficult challenges for me was learning how to solve word problems. But with the Chandlers' help, I was able to filter through the scheme and learn how to use the information provided to solve word problems. And during the last semester of my senior year I passed (and conquered!) that final TAAS math test. Don't ask me what I made because I no longer remember. I just know that I passed the exam. I thank God that my mom drove me back and forth to my tutoring sessions, and I am forever grateful to Pastor and Sister Chandler for opening up their home to me and tutoring me for free for nearly four years. I had been taking advanced placement classes my junior and senior years so not only did I graduate, I graduated with honors. There were one hundred and four students in my graduation class at Giddings High School and fifty-one of us graduated with honors.

I believe God is with each of us even before we dream of being born, but how we interpret and describe His presence in our lives is different for each of us. There's no right or wrong way for us to experience that relationship. We simply each have our own unique relationship with Him. Since I was a young child, probably around the time I was in kindergarten, I have known what God looks like and what He feels like to me. God isn't black, God isn't white, God isn't brown. God has been around way before religion was brought into the equation, so, in my mind, God isn't Baptist, Catholic, Presbyterian, or Methodist. God isn't a Muslim, a Jew or a Christian. God, above all things, first is Love. To truly experience the power of God is to love, without judgment, with unreserved feelings, just to love and love and love and then love some more, fully. I felt it in the depths of my heart and I don't know where it came from. I just knew what I felt in my soul—wherever there is love, there is God, and wherever there is God, there is love. The most powerful and sacred thing of all was knowing I had a choice to love or not to love. And I knew that God wasn't going to make that choice for me.

I chose to be baptized when I was eight years old. On that morning, just as on every previous Sunday morning, there was a row of empty chairs waiting at the front of the church. But on this particular Sunday, I felt a burning sensation in my body as I looked at those familiar chairs. It was a feeling in my body that told me to get up and move when Pastor Chandler "opened the doors" of the church to anyone who wanted to accept God as the Lord and Savior of his or her life and to accept membership in the church. I felt a fire in me as I looked at the usher standing behind one of the empty chairs. I moved. I answered all the questions the church clerk asked me. Never wanting to feel left out, my cousin Pumpkin jumped up and sat in the open chair beside me, and a few weeks later we were both baptized. However, I did not truly become saved until many years later.

From day one I have had strong, God-fearing, loving women in my family. On my dad's side of the family, my great-great-grandmother, Grandma Mila, lived to be a hundred and two. She began to lose her eyesight because of glaucoma when she was ninety-two. I would go with my great-grandfather to visit her and even though she could not see me with her physical eyes, she loved me. Her hands were as soft as the skin of a newborn and as smooth as silk. Her skin was light brown and I could feel it loosely slide back and forth across her knuckles as she caressed my tiny hands. I would sit in a chair beside her bed and she would ask me to move closer to her so she could touch my face and hear my voice. Within seconds she would know which little twig I was on the family tree. Her love was so pure. Then she would make me recite the alphabet and as I began with A, B, C, she would make me slow down to make sure I was pronouncing each letter correctly. After fifteen or twenty minutes I was ready to go back outside and play, but not before I leaned in real close to get a kiss and a slight bite on my cheek.

I still remember the night they called to tell us Grandma Mila had passed. It was a warm summer night. I was five. My great-grandparents and I went to the house where Grandma Mila had lived with her daughter and waited for the ambulance to come and get her body. I went into her room one last time and as I looked at her still body lying so peaceful on her bed, I cupped my hands over hers. I could still feel the love she had always expressed towards me as I said, "Good-bye, Grandma Mila. Thank you for teaching me how to say my ABCs."

When an elder in my family prophesied that something was going to come to pass, the prophecy was received as the truth. An older person was considered wise and was respected for knowing the word of God. Elders spoke from the soul with words of faith and experience and their words were not questioned. A prophecy usually included the words, "God put this on my heart to share with you...."

One day when I was around seven years old, I was playing in the living room at my Bear Mama's house. Bear Mamma was my mom's mom. My mom, Kathy, and my aunt Judy were watching television and my Bear Mamma was relaxing in a recliner as she watched my cousin Pumpkin, my older brother Dywarne and me play. We finally got tired of playing in the house and as we stood up to go outside, my Bear Mama said, "Kathy, you know J is going to make a fine pastor when he grows up." I stopped and turned around. Bear Mama looked at me and said, "Baby, you are going to make a fine pastor when you get older."

My Aunt Judy said, "J is too bad to be a pastor."

Bear Mama replied, "Never mind all of that. He is going to be a real good preacher. God put that on my heart to share with you, baby." My mom just smiled, but I remember feeling confused and afraid.

Oddly enough, a few weeks later, Big Mama, my great-grandmother on my dad's side of the family, told me one afternoon while I was lying on the floor watching cartoons, "J, you are going to be a good speaker when you get older. God is really going to use you. He put that one in my heart to share with you." These two women shared with me the exact same vision but it wasn't until I was sixteen or seventeen that I told them they each had made the same prophecy.

When the Lord prophesied to Abraham that Sarah would have a baby, even though they both were well into old age, she laughed because she could not conceive that such an event could occur. Just like Sarah, I laughed at the visions these two beautiful women saw regarding my future. I laughed partly out of doubt and partly out of fear. I wasn't afraid of doing God's will. I was afraid of doing it and not getting it right. I was afraid He might use a red ink pen to circle the wrong words and underline the incorrect actions! I began to have an internal dialog downplaying what these two women shared with me. I went so far as to try and convince myself that they were wrong.

Most of us have done this to ourselves at one time or another.

Someone shares a vision for our lives with us, or we have our own vision, and instead of allowing ourselves to grow toward and become the vision, we find ways to convince ourselves that we're not good enough. Instead of focusing on our possibilities and affirming, "I can do all things through Christ Jesus who strengthens me," we focus on our limitations. We tune into our inner critic. Channing Pollock said, "A critic is a legless man who teaches running." Are you aware of your inner critic? We all have this voice that tells us we are bad, stupid, clumsy, and cowardly. Although its intent is to help us succeed, the harsh talk of the inner critic just serves to drain our energy and lower our morale and our immune system.

To defuse the inner critic, we need to recognize when it is speaking. We need to realize that this voice does not speak for who we really are or what we really want to do, and that listening to this inner critic is an old pattern that has never really served us. We can ask ourselves, "Are these words helpful?" "What supportive thoughts do I choose to think instead?" Donald A. Laird said, "Abilities wither under faultfinding, blossom with encouragement."

Sometimes we unconsciously self-sabotage the destiny that God has offered us, as we focus on the negative and not on the positive aspects of His will and vision. And sometimes we self-sabotage on purpose. We rebel.

I was once told "You can think good things are going to happen or you can think bad things are going to happen. Either way, you won't be disappointed." I would rather think good thoughts and be right half of the time than think bad thoughts and be right all of the time. Wouldn't you?

Chapter 2
Conforming

"For my thoughts are not your thoughts, neither are your ways my ways, declares the Lord. As the heavens are higher than the earth, so are my ways higher than your ways and my thoughts than your thoughts." -Isaiah 55:8-9 (NIV Bible)

I have been in the favor of the Lord from the moment I was conceived, but I have been trying to gain the acceptance of the world my entire life. I once heard Pastor Jones, my pastor and friend, say, "Running with the world doesn't make you more Christian, but more worldly." I remember back to when I was a young child and my grandmothers shared with me the vision the Lord had given them for my life. I started doing the opposite of what He wanted me to do, even though my desire to be a speaker lit my soul on fire. He was asking me to lead and I was choosing to run the other direction. I was more comfortable with the idea of doing what *I* thought I was supposed to do than with conforming to what God was telling me to do.

To be perfectly honest, I still struggle with this today. (I actually wrote this chapter last because what I need to say strips me down to my very core.) Sometimes I have to step back and ask myself, "Which do I love more, the gift or the Giver of the gift?" I have observed many people struggling against the waves of life, trying to live life their way and on their terms instead of allowing the ebb and flow of the ocean to support themselves.

Mother Teresa, a globally beloved example of saintly devotion to the poor, spent the last fifty years of her life struggling with doubts about her faith. Sixty-six years' worth of deeply personal letters to her superiors and confessors are included in the recently published book, *Mother Teresa: Come Be My Light.* "If there be God—please forgive me. When I try to raise my thoughts to Heaven, there is such convicting emptiness that those very thoughts return like sharp knives and hurt my very soul," she wrote. "How painful is this unknown pain—I have no Faith." In the 1960s, after receiving an important prize, she wrote, "This means nothing to me because I don't have Him."

"I've never read a saint's life where the saint has such an intense spiritual darkness," said Father Kolodiejchuk, author of *Mother Teresa: Come Be My Light.* Many believers suffer from crises of faith, but the duration of Teresa's alienation from Christ seems extreme. It began, she said, soon after she set up her Missionaries of Charity in Calcutta in the late 1940s to succor India's poor. And it lasted, with only a joyous five-week respite in 1959 when she re-found God, until her death at age eighty-seven, a decade ago. "There is such terrible darkness within me, as if everything was dead. It has been like this more or less from the time I started 'the work,'" she wrote in 1953.

Conforming can be defined as being obedient to our inner vision of what we want from life. The Bible says, "Do not conform yourselves to the standards of this world, but let God transform you inwardly by a complete change of your mind. Then you will be able to know the will of God." Whether I wanted to admit it or not, I always had a vision for my life, and I give all the credit to my great-grandparents and my two grandmothers for encouraging me to not just settle for whatever was handed to me.

Being on a farm is hard work. On my great-grandparents'

farm, during the summers we would haul hay and during the winters we would bust and sell firewood. I learned some very important lessons while spending time with my great-grandparents. I learned that hard work reaps its own rewards. My reward was realizing that I was not a fan of manual labor! I definitely knew that whatever I was eventually going to do with my life, I would much rather have a career using my mental muscles than busting my back and wearing out my knees doing manual labor. Along with that came the awareness that if I wanted a choice in what I was going to do for a living, I was going to have to graduate from high school and go on to earn a college degree.

Another thing I learned at a very young age during those summers on the farm was to ride a horse. In fact, I became so good at it that my great-grandfather let me help him break the horses that were too wild to be ridden. The more experience I gained, the cockier I became. One day while some of my cousins and I were getting ready to go on a trail ride, I jumped on the back. of a horse we called Jo Jo, without a saddle or a good bridle, and I quickly felt the pain of my arrogance. Jo Jo broke out running down a dirt road and bucking until I fell off and broke my right arm.

Just because we are good at something, be it riding horses or waiting on tables in a restaurant, it doesn't mean we should show it less respect, practice it less or feel that it owes us something. The minute we begin to think this way, we become careless and mistakes are going to be made. I remember hearing Chris Rock sharing a story on TV about when he had his HBO show. He could hear the band Aerosmith on another studio set rehearsing for an appearance on the David Letterman show and these guys were going through each song like it was their first gig. I mean, this was Aerosmith and these guys had been making hits for over twenty years! However, they knew the importance of not taking anything for granted. A quality, I'm sure, that helped them reach a very high level of success. If we feel we are owed something so badly that we stop doing things the right way, then maybe it's time to reevaluate what is really important. I am not saying I am a master horseman but I felt I was good enough to become careless and, unfortunately for me, I had to break my arm in order to learn a painful but life-enhancing lesson.

Conforming also means being obedient to your true self and not basing your identity on what other people think. For example, people will tell you if you are tall and have big hands, you should play basketball; if you are quick and agile, you should play football, and if you are funny, you should be a comedian. When I was in the fifth grade I saw *Mo' Better Blues*, directed by Spike Lee, a movie about a very talented trumpet player named Bleak Gilliam. After watching *Mo' Better Blues*, I decided I wanted to learn how to play the trumpet, so when I entered the sixth grade I signed up for band. I was eager to learn to play the trumpet like Bleak, but also I wasn't allowed to play sports until the seventh grade and band was the next best way to show your school spirit. Another reason I wanted to join band was because I really liked Mr. Spooner, the band instructor. After meeting with him just one time, he made me feel like being in the band was the place to be.

So my mom and I went to the band hall a few weeks before school was to start to sign me up for trumpet lessons. Imagine my surprise and disappointment when I discovered Mr. Spooner no longer worked at the school. He had been replaced by Mr. Nelson and his assistant, Ms. Dyer. There were several kids looking around the band room trying to decide which instrument they wanted to play. I remember Ms. Dyer asking me which instrument I wanted to play. I responded, "The trumpet," with a million-dollar smile on my face.

Ms. Dyer put a trumpet mouthpiece against my lips and said, "Blow." Then she said, "Your lips are too big to play the trumpet. You need to play the baritone."

I said, "I don't want to play the baritone. I want to learn how to play the trumpet."

"Well," Ms. Dyer said, "all the chairs in the trumpet section are filled. We need you to learn how to play the baritone."

I was crushed. I didn't remember seeing any baritone solos in *Mo' Better Blues*. I went from feeling like "Mr. Cool" to feeling out of place. I went from being able to carry a slick trumpet case around to having to carry a beat-up case for my baritone that looked like a suitcase. More importantly, I went from thinking band was the place to be to wishing I could drop out of band. I played the baritone the entire time I was in junior high and I hated every minute of it. Whenever I took it home with me, I would have to struggle with getting that beat-up case up the steps of the bus. Then I would have to sit at the first open seat I could find, and I had to sit by myself because the baritone case left no room for another person. Going to the back of the bus to hang out with my friends was not an option because it was impossible to slide that case down the bus aisle. I remember practicing in my backyard after school only to hear a neighbor tell my mom to PLEASE STOP me from playing because the sound was something awful and her husband was trying to get some sleep before going in to work the graveyard shift!

I dreaded going to band class every day. It was almost as bad as being asked to read out loud. Mr. Nelson was loud and he would go into these childish temper tantrums if the class practice wasn't going well. His office had a glass window and he would storm into his office whenever he got pissed off and we could see him in there, screaming and yelling. Ms. Dyer was rude and

31

always criticizing us. I failed band one semester with a 62 and had to sit out half of my seventh grade football season until I brought my grade up. When I graduated from the eighth grade, I was finished with band.

Deep down inside I felt I had betrayed myself by signing up for band. I had signed up even though I knew Mr. Spooner wouldn't be there, even though I didn't want to play the baritone and even though I didn't have to be there. I had signed up because I wanted to be like a character in a movie. I had not been true to myself.

I have learned that conforming is a sign of strength, a sign of mature, spiritual growth. More specifically, conforming involves learning to set boundaries, especially between ourselves and life's distractions. The anonymous authors of a book of daily meditations, *Answers in the Heart*, said it best: "Starting to set boundaries for ourselves takes time and practice. Because the experience is unfamiliar, we may often find ourselves veering between two extremes—holding back for the fear of blurring our boundaries or acting as if we have no boundaries at all. But our willingness to set boundaries and stick with them brings us a clearer sense of who we are. We begin to learn where we start and end. We start to learn the same about other people. With boundaries comes a new sense of self-respect because they are our affirmations to ourselves that we are not objects to be trampled on or used, but we are human beings with dignity."

Some boundaries are meant to be stretched, such as learning to ride a bicycle without the training wheels or trusting a seventeen-year-old teenager to watch after her younger siblings without destroying the house. However, some boundaries are never meant to be stretched and if you do and live to tell about it, you were simply playing Russian roulette. For example, I have stretched the boundaries of the law by driving under the influence of a controlled substance. I have stretched the boundaries of common sense by participating in unprotected sex. There is no excuse for either behavior and I am certainly not boasting. I have even stretched the boundaries of the Ten Commandments by trying to be cool with my friends and joining them in activities which were illegal. When I was in high school I went to a house party and got into some serious trouble for stealing. I was walking out of the master bedroom bathroom when I saw some guys rummaging through the drawer of a night stand next to the bed. Just as I was about to leave the room, one of the guys found a bag full of one-hundred-dollar bills. I never should have looked back, but I did. The guys begin grabbing handfuls of money and one of them asked me if I wanted some. Ernest Hemingway said, "Courage is grace under pressure." It takes real courage to walk away when temptation is staring you right in the face. I didn't. I said yes. A couple of days passed and then I heard that the news going around was that three thousand dollars had been stolen from the parents of the girl who had thrown the party. For the next couple of weeks, every time my phone rang, I just knew it was the police. The other guys were all trying to get their stories together. Most of them had already spent the stolen money on PlayStations, shoes, clothes, and other stuff.

I remember taking two hundred dollars. I had a tire blow out as I was leaving the party so I used seventy bucks to get a new tire for my car. I remember feeling like I could afford anything. Having the money to pay for a new tire made me feel like I was an adult. Nothing could have been further from the truth. I had a gut feeling that I was about to get into a world of trouble, so I put the rest of the money in the ashtray of my car. A couple of days later I was called to the principal's office where I was greeted by a police officer. He began to ask me questions about the party. I knew the best thing for me was to fess up, and I did. We went

JONATHAN OLIVER

out to my car and I gave the officer the rest of the money. After school, I had to drive downtown and fill out a formal confession. All I could think about was how was I going to break the news to my mom. Well, I didn't have to worry about that for long because as she was driving home from work she saw my car at the police station. One the officers told me that my mom was just outside the door and I remember thinking "Not *my* mom, you must have her confused with someone else." But it was her. She came into the office and as I made my confession, my mom listened to every word while big tears rolled down her face.

I no longer felt like I was the big man who could afford anything. I felt like a coward. Only a coward would steal to get ahead and break the heart of his mother along the way. When I left the police station my mom told me she was disappointed in me, however, her love for me was stronger than ever because I hadn't lied to the police, I had given back the money, and I had been very cooperative. No charges were pressed against me. I did have to write a letter of apology to the owners of the house and I was kicked off the basketball team and placed on two years' probation. But the consequences of my actions could have been a lot worse. Today, as I look back at that incident from the vantage point of maturity, I can clearly see how that experience and many others of my youth were teaching me to be true to myself. By experiencing what I didn't want, I knew better what I really wanted out of life. If we pay attention, I feel life shows us what direction we need to go or the next move we need to make. But to get what we really want out of life, we have to let go of the old before we can move on to the new. Letting go has never been easy for me—too much sadness and hurt feelings. For most people, as we are growing up, there is no discussion about how to deal with the sadness, the feelings of hurt and the loneliness that are sometimes part of making a choice or a move. We ignore our shadows with overly enthusiastic excitement for the new. I think it all comes down to surrendering to the bigger picture.

When my older brother had left for college, we began to drift apart. I can't really put a finger on why that happened. It may have been because we have a four-year age difference and we were just hanging out with different people. But when my older brother left, I still had my little brother at home with me, and the bond between us got stronger. We did have different fathers and there were times during our childhood when I felt bad because we didn't always get to experience the same things, like when I got to go to Astroworld and he didn't. When he was nine, I remember asking him if he had ever been to a movie theater and he told me he hadn't. So, on his tenth birthday, I took him to the movie theater and we watched our first movie together, *Rookie of the Year*. We celebrated his birthday in this way for the next two years. And then the next year I didn't take him to the movies because I was being selfish, hanging out with my friends and thinking I was too cool for that. Later my mom told me that my behavior really hurt my brother's feelings. When I allow my mind to go back to that time in my life, I almost come to tears because I should have taken him to the movies that year. Today we have a strong, loving friendship and a close brotherly relationship. My younger brother will always have a place in my heart. The love I have for him is impeccable.

When I left for college I had to say goodbye to the little boy in me, the sense of innocence, and the comfort of living in the same town for the first eighteen years of my life. And I especially regretted letting go of living with my younger brother. He was twelve, I was eighteen, and I wished we had more time to share together. College was only four hours away, but we both knew things would be different. We cried our hearts out as we said our goodbyes and I cried for the next two hours as I drove down the highway. As I conform to the person I am becoming, I still struggle with letting go—letting go of relationships and old habits that no longer serve me.

My true feelings tell me that what conforming ultimately comes down to is balance. Jakob Wasserman said, "In every person, even in such that appear most reckless, there is an inherent desire to attain balance." Someone once said, "Only when we can love hell will we find heaven." People often view the spiritual path as a search for the light. In truth, spirituality asks us to bring light and darkness together in wholeness. And, in fact, this is the only possible solution. In our world of duality, any effort to focus all attention on the light only serves to increase the power of the darkness. Our aim is not to deny or reject anything but to embrace it all. Martia Nelson said, "When you are able to contain both the light and dark together, that is a very enlightening state. It means that you no longer have to choose one experience over another. You do not have to choose love OR hate, blame OR forgiveness, sadness OR joy, anger OR openheartedness. You are no longer polarized; no particular feeling boxes you in and keeps you from the light of true self. You then have access to the full range of human experiences you came into this life to embrace."

It has been said that the light of God is so bright that it appears as darkness to us. When we feel we're living in darkness, we may be living in the all-encompassing light of God's love and compassion for struggle. We must be willing to struggle, to fall down, stumble around, and make mistakes. We must be in tune with the constant process of death and rebirth that is part of life's rhythm. It's in YOU. Each of us has an internal timetable—the rhythm of our spirit. Discovering what that rhythm is and conforming to it can bring us untold serenity and joy. The ability to conform brings us energy, replacing the energy we used up while fighting against ourselves. So often we are our own worst enemy.

But to face who we are and to learn from it, is to be created anew. In the process, we discover our own truths. Maybe that's part of what a spiritual awakening is, seeing the truth in a new way.

Chapter 3
Compliments

"You [are like] unfaithful wives [having illicit love affairs with the world and breaking your marriage vow to God!] Do you not know that being the world's friend is being God's enemy? So whoever chooses to be a friend of the world takes his stand as an enemy of God." -James 4:4 (AMP)

"I can live for two months on a good compliment." -Mark Twain

"Men are more accountable for their motives than for anything else." -Archibald Alexander

To discern whether a compliment is worthy of your acceptance, you must examine the context in which it is taken. All compliments are not good compliments.

Except for my current girlfriend, Saran, I have never been faithful to any woman I was dating or with whom I was having sexual relations. Except for one person, I have never been loyal to anyone, not even myself. And that is sad. The cause of my behavior? I think it was the compliments. I liked the way they stroked my ego. They filled my chest full of pride and arrogance. They made me feel accepted. The question I have had to learn to ask myself upon receiving a compliment is: If I accept this compliment will I have compromised my integrity just to have my ego stroked? If I haven't, then I can simply say thank you and continue living my life according to God's will.

Actually, compliments have had a detrimental effect on all areas of my life at one time or another. For example, there have been times where just as I was preparing to put in my two weeks on a job, my boss or a coworker would give me a compliment. Like a drug, that simple compliment magically made everything seem right with the world. The result: I have stayed with jobs six months longer than I wanted to because of the compliments given to me during an average day! And, often, it didn't matter to me if my behavior, after receiving a compliment from another person, caused pain in someone else's life. I was very selfish.

I have also stayed in many personal relationships longer than I should have, mainly because I was told I was good in bed. For me, compliments have been even harder to evaluate when they are of a sexual nature. In past relationships, I would fall in love with the sex, but swear up and down that it was an intimate relationship. Dating for me has been easy, but once sex was involved and my ego begin to get fed, then sex would quickly become intimacy and intimacy meant love.

I once broke a golden commandment to God and to myself. I was involved in an affair with a married woman. I knew that I was playing with fire and given my religious beliefs and morals, not to mention common sense, I just should have known better. In all actuality, I did know better. My involvement with this woman started while she was going through an on-again, off-again relationship with her fiancé. The flirting begun innocently enough, but our relationship quickly became a sexual one. Now, this person was not asking for a commitment from me. Neither was she giving me one. But I owed it to myself to have treated Jonathan with more respect and dignity even if she had wanted comfort in a time of need. The point is this: given the egotistical and self-centered person that I was at that time, I was drawn to this woman like an addict in need of a fix. Because the compliments had a more powerful influence over me than the sex, I used them to justify my behavior. I rationalized it all in my head when I should have simply listened to my heart. And this very selfish way of thinking is what is causing heartache and pain in many relationships today.

So the dating continued for a couple of years during her engagement. After she married we both agreed that we should stop seeing each other for obvious reasons and we did, for a while. But remember what I said about compliments, ego, and addiction. Well, things begin to get a little slippery if you know what I mean and before long her compliments started whispering in my ear and I was eager to respond because I saw myself as of the world and not a child of God in the world. Thus, I had an affair with a married woman.

It's not the woman's fault. She was only a person speaking the feelings that she felt. But I am Jonathan James Oliver and I am the one who must own my choices and actions, good or bad. I am the one who must remain in integrity and be accountable with myself first before I can expect to be faithful and true to someone else.

Compliments are merely words. But when I was giving in, reaching out and making choices in hopes of receiving compliments, that's when they became a need. That need nearly cost me my life. Not as in I was almost killed, but as in I almost lost who I was inside. My secret, intimate relationship with God was threatened, and, for me, that kind of separation from God, well, I was on the verge of dying a spiritual death and that is the worst death I could have possibly had; the death that comes from my soul not being nourished. When I have let compliments affect my live in a negative way, I was not being honest with Jonathan. So, be true to yourself. Be honest with yourself.

The insanity of my addiction:
It's May 10, 2005, about 12:42 a.m. and I am just going to start by just putting it out there on the table. I need to start making positive positive positive changes in my life I am just very unhappy right now with my actions what I have been doing in my life. I feel like I can do better right now in my life I feel separated from God today is just a bad day on a bad day like today I'm feeling like I haven't prayed a real strong prayer I haven't prayed a real prayer of focus on a day like today I can feel myself just really beating up on myself. I can feel me just being a little too hard on myself for being upset with myself I am going to take that into consideration. Richard Carlson, author of *Don't Sweat the Small Stuff*, wrote if you ask a person on a good day how everything is going before they go to work everything is great the wife is beautiful the kids are geniuses the car drives perfect everything is awesome then when they come in from work the wife is a nag the kids are stupid you drive a piece of crap, it all depends on what kind of mood are you in at the time I guess right now I am not in a good mood some of these matters may seem negative or depressing that I am writing about right now. I have not worked out in about three weeks; I feel very uncomfortable and bloated. I have some mail that I need to take care of college consolidation loan papers my planner for the week is not organized basically there are some things that I need to do to help me put everything in a good perspective; I need to make some important phone calls some motivational phone calls people that I need to speak with as far as my career instead I just have been polluting my mind. How do I say no to things that I know I should not be doing preferably women dating women just say no and I

have not been saying no. I have been very selfish and very hypocritical of myself. The public my grandmother my mom, and my dad none of them know but the fact that I know is enough in itself. I just thank God that He keeps me in His grace I just thank God God I thank you for keeping me in your grace God I thank you for just loving me while I am covered in my self pity. Thank you for loving me Jesus thank you for just allowing me to continue to push forward for just allowing me to continue to push forward. Right now I feel that I am going through an internal spiritual war for the control of my mind not my mind like I am going crazy or losing my sanity; I am talking about my mind as far as surrendering and making a sacrifice to God's will every day I feel like I have to make a sacrifice if not every day I know at least every other week I am making a personal sacrifice if I don't stay on top of this thing I can easily get off track and when I get off track it kills me. Some of it is just embarrassment that I got off track and it just pisses me off I feel like I have already screwed up so I might as well just go all out and screw up more and that pisses me off; I have messed up I haven't done what I thought I would be doing I haven't made the improvement that I thought I was going to be making. I have prayed these long prayers to God and have asked Him for all of these great blessings and I still find a way to mess it all up I still find a way to not get it right even after I have prayed for a long time and I have asked God to forgive me and to bless me and I have told Him how I want to do better thanking and praising Him praying for thirty minutes those have been some of my best moments some of the times I have felt the greatest but two weeks later I am back in the same boat and I am praying the same prayer again I feel like I have not made any improvements. Sometimes I feel like the devil just comes at me even harder he comes at me even more when he sees me collapsing on my knees; he sees me just throwing my hands up in

43

the air just saying ok God I'm yours I'm yours I'm yours I'm yours for whatever you want me to do. The devil has his head turned and he is screwing with someone else's life; he hears me make that call out to God and then he is like ooh let me get back over here and mess with Jonathan by godly look Jonathan is trying to act like he wants to do something positive; he thinks he has this thing beat so let me get over there and distract him real quick. And before I know it I am back into feeling uncomfortable again or I'm depressed again knowing that I have not done what I thought I was going to do or I hadn't stuck to my prayer praying like I was going to and I know it bothers and upsets me especially with me wanting to be an inspirational motivational speaker I can't even keep myself motivated let alone try to motivate thousands of people. I'm coming to realize that once I've learned to master myself in that arena that of its own gives me wisdom so once I can do that and do it repeatedly then God will have me to be of more help to someone else I just really honest to god believe that. Right now it is funny how people on the outside view me they don't really know what is going on with me and if they wanted to they would ask and sometimes they really don't want to know because they are dealing with things of their own so the last thing they need to deal with or hear is something going on with me I'm not trying to be rude about it they would rather not even ask and not asking is basically saying I don't want to know. If I 'm not dead and I have a job and whatever then evidently I am doing just fine sometimes I think that's the way my father thinks about me. It bothers me that we don't get along or we don't talk that much anymore like we used to we used to talk all the time three or four times a week and sometimes thirty forty minutes at a time now we talk every other week maybe five or ten minutes and the conversation is so fake I like to call it a credential conversation we speak in credentials nothing of a substance more as did you see the game I'm going out of town and stuff like that never a real good solid conversation. My mom and I bless her heart sometimes if it was not for her being that other parent I feel like I would be completely alone. It's going to come a point when I will be like that but while I have them here in good health and right mind I'd like to be able to experience them both to the fullest that's just not what's going to happen for us right now. My mom and I at one point were not as close as we are but we still had that spiritual connection to one another. Now it's starting to become more in sync with the body and mind as well as spiritual it's powerful it's not like that at all with my father. It never really has been a spiritual connection with my father, but at least we had the mind set at one point now we don't even have that anymore. I feel as if I must just put everything out on the table my addiction is going to kill me if I don't give it over to God my sex addiction my sex addiction is going to kill me if I don't give it over to God. I am absolutely powerless to it and that's just the bottom line my sex addiction if I do not give it over to God is going to take my life it will take my life first off by just making me miserable for not being in control of my own life. I think about sex when I don't even *want* to think about it. It hurts me sometimes when sex enters my mind sex sometimes enters into my mind and it just creeps me out to even think about it because I have lusted over it for so long it is a curse to even imagine it. I am glad that I am writing right now glad that I am exhausting myself by admitting it. Writing right now is like conversing with my mind out loud I have just been miserable with this sex addiction and with being a sex addict it is literally a drug. Today I felt like I was in and out on an emotional high as if I felt drunk but when I am sober it is such a marvelous thing. My goal is just to work on it today to take it one day at a time to take it one day at a time to take it just one day at a time and to seize the day. I don't want to get to the point where I am just so go go go and not meditating to where I just succumb to the addiction again need to keep my Higher Power at the tip of my nose so that my eyes can focus on it and realize that I am a sex addict and there are no ifs ands or buts about it. I am beginning to realize that thinking is not doing; just because I think about sex does not mean I have to have sex just thinking about masturbating does not mean I have to masturbate every time I get arousal does not mean I have to touch it. It is ok to have not have masturbated in a month. I know that "I" do not want God to give me a wife or anyone special in my life with all of this junk inside of me right now I know that I need to clean up the inside of my mind before I can allow another person to enter my life. I believe wholeheartedly in my heart that I would not ever be happy with anyone in my life until I am completely able to sell myself out and love God above and beyond anything and everything. He has blessed me with this beautiful gift and I feel like I am just wasting it on sex; I have just been screwing around literally it's not fun I don't even enjoy it just having sex with someone because they have a beautiful body or because we had a great conversation that doesn't even build up enough commitment in the soul to enjoy it not to mention that this isn't the way it is supposed to be enjoyed anyway unless there is a ring on her finger and yours. I know God is a merciful God I believe that I just do not want to lose the spiritual gift that God has blessed me with because I haven't spoken to Him with it God I don't want to lose my spiritual gift that you have blessed me with and forgive me for not speaking through it to you I love you. I love you Jesus I love you for so many reasons I love you for just allowing me to say I love you to you I love you for just allowing me to have the mind set to be able to write boldly about myself to call myself out to say you know what J. you are screwing around too much you're jacking around too much and you need to get your stuff in gear buddy. I have some habits that are going to cripple and kill me at a young age first spiritually then mentally and finally physically if I don't change them and everything I want to experience living on a coast having a boat driving a Lamborghini and all those other beautiful blessings blessings that God can bless me with simply out of the sheer fact that God is a gracious God my wildest dreams will not even come close if I don't do what He asks me to do. If God just surprisingly decided to bless me by just being who He is and He can make that decision I would not be able to even enjoy those blessings fully knowing that I did not receive them the way that He really wanted me to have them. This goes with sex as well so much of this is that I am unhappy with my family. I am going to start writing *Impersonations* this week DaRhonda says that I should begin by writing chapter three first and I pray God that this is your will that I begin with chapter three. If it is not your will I ask you to bless me with what chapter I should begin writing first. I ask you God to help change my eating habit in a way that I am able to focus on you; if it calls for fasting from certain things then I will fast for you God. I can't make up for yesterday I can't make up for all the jacking around I did on Monday but on Tuesday I know that I can come into your grace I know that I am always in your grace but I also know I can begin to walk a different path I feel better just writing this right now God. This is real this thing is real. I love you Jesus and I just pray that I am able to do your will to the fullest not groggily but full heartedly. I just feel a real distance my father and I do not talk that much my older brother and I talk but we are not in that groove yet; my little brother and I are in that groove. I may not agree with him about something and he does not agree with me on everything but we still respect one another; my older brother and my father feel I am challenging them if I don't agree with them just because I have a different perspective on some things. Another thing all of a sudden I'm grown not grown in the sense that that was an intelligent thought you just shared and I like the way you are thinking and here's another idea but grown in the sense that I am accused of being a smart ass because I did not agree with them. Or they don't want to speak to me anymore because I am too grown to hear what they have to say. It bothers me that I am limited in my ability to fully communicate with my older brother and my father I want to be able to communicate openly and when there is something on which we don't agree that's fine out of respect for each other we can agree to disagree. Today I felt so bad for a little while like I wasn't going to make it but I knew I was one thing that is just amazing; I feel like God is protecting me for a particular reason. No matter how hard I try to screw it up He will get done what He is trying to accomplish hopefully hopefully I will see it accomplished before my mind is completely taken away by my sex addiction. It is as if God is telling me it is His will for me to accomplish this task for Him and not only accomplish it but grow spiritually during the process but if in God's eyes I have not grown spiritually if I did not learn or comprehend what He wanted me to while accomplishing His will then I am forever out of His grace. It is by God's grace that I am here. Speeding throughout Houston and not getting into an accident is God's grace driving drunk and not killing someone or my self is by God's grace He is saving me for a particular task! All of this grace that I am sucking up while thinking that I am cool or that I can't be touched or that I am getting away with something is going to come back full circle in my face if I don't surrender completely to God's will that's the bottom line. This make-believe church that I have in my head reading my Bible at my own convenience praying at my own convenience repenting at my own convenience is all crap and not even remotely pleasing to God because it is all done at my convenience. It should be done at His will it's not about me! Even though I make a mistake I know I don't need to beat myself up curse myself out or fear that God is going to kill me but I also know when I am getting away with too much that's when I try to convince myself with one of those stupid clichés like it's ok everyone else is doing it if there's anything I know it's don't lie to Jonathan. The worst thing I can do is start judging myself against that old bull crap believing it. So I leave the make-believe church and I pick up my Bible and I know that the wisdom I find there has passed the test of time it is Law it is the Word it is there to be read spoken and obeyed not to be twisted tweaked or compromised in order to ease the pain of what I am going through *Impersonations* is what I need to get started on because writing this book is going to open my eyes to a lot of things that I need to see for myself; this is going to help begin the healing of some relationships with my family for my family's sake while these people are still in their right mind while we may still be able to grab hold of just a little understanding. As God allows me and my family members to improve then the healing can spread out into the world where God is already using me to work wonders but as I grow spiritually in my process and accomplish God's will then I will completely experience God's grace and all of the blessings He has in store for me; I will be unable to even speak about the goodness of the Lord without falling down on my knees giving Him praise and glory. Don't act out I go in there and I begin to feel powerless depressed embarrassed ashamed I'm turning on the computer hunting for porn I begin to get a fake high which never lasts long enough. All of those feelings begin to rush back into my head only now they cause me to feel ten times worse powerless depressed embarrassed ashamed. I begin to feel insecure and not worthy of anything good or positive to doubt my relationship with God

Saran with everyone. I become completely isolated and alone so I continue to act out I continue to watch the porn and I masturbate because it keeps me momentarily from dealing with the aftermath of my acting out. Everything in my life right then is unmanageable and I am almost completely unfocused with no concern for the future with no thought about the past. Finally when I am completely tired of masturbating and have watched the same porn over and over again when all of it has become a big blur I stop I feel powerless depressed embarrassed ashamed very insecure alone unworthy angry separate from God I am in this familiar huge dark pit from which I have to climb out all over again. I feel scared and the porn I have been watching over the last hours begins to haunt my thoughts I try to catch back up with time but I can't. My relationships with God Saran family friends begin to feel distanced I am depressed for the rest of the day.

Moving On

One day at a time, keep it simple, progress not perfection, H.A.L.T., stick with winners, conceive the blessings God wants me to have, talk with my sponsor, live and let God, I know what to do, I don't want to act out, I battle with this every day.

Yesterday I bought the new SAA Big Book and I thought that I was in the clear. As I write I have come to realize that I am absolutely powerless over my addiction. Every day for the rest of my life I will be a recovering sex addict. To put blinders over my eyes and think that one day I will be in the clear only sets me up for a long and painful fall from grace. I must learn how to channel my emotions and feelings into a safer environment. I am tried of running after time when I have spent hours acting out. Admitting that I am completely powerless and that I can not will my sex addiction will help me to completely surrender it over to God. I know what I am afraid of. I am afraid that once I let my sex addiction go, there will be no more excuses and that comfort which I run to will no longer be there, a safe place waiting for me. Yes, I am afraid. I am afraid of not having my addiction. But I am more afraid of my addiction having me and destroying me. So that so-called safe environment is now going to be replaced with faith. That makes me afraid also because I don't know all of the answers, but it is a healthier kind of fear.

There are lessons to be learned from every experience, good or bad. I must be willing to stop thinking about my fear, and open myself to be teachable. I have learned that sex addition isn't really about sex. The sex is just the tip of the iceberg. I am using the sex as a cover-up to hide from my honest feelings. I am using the porn, hiding behind it instead of facing fear, stress, or reality.

The three important lessons I have learned about my sex addiction are, first, recovery is a 24 hours/7-days-a-week full-time job. I can't let go of the present moment when the sun goes down just because I was sober during the day. Also, what may have worked for my recovery during the day may not work for me at night. It is not easy. It takes courage, hope, and faith. Some stressful moments may pass as I take a deep breath and others may need more—calling on God, support groups, family, or friends.

Second, during my recovery I must learn to trust myself completely so that I can let go and trust the process.

Finally, I have learned I must have patience with myself and with my compulsive behavior. There are times when I feel like nothing is happening. I'm just in recovery, moving at a snail's pace. No matter what pace I am moving at, as long as it is in recovery that's all that matters. Just like the snail must feel, at times I feel I'm not making any progress but when I look back I suddenly realize I have crossed the street.

There comes a day when we each realize that looking for

external solutions to problems will not work. Here are some tools that I have used to help me believe in myself and rely less on the words of others. Make a Gratitude List. Making a list of things I am grateful for keeps me more balanced. Do something nice for someone else and don't tell anyone about it. Read. I love to read motivational books. Among my favorites are *Live Your Dreams* by Les Brown, *The 21 Irrefutable Laws of Leadership* and *The 21 Indispensable Qualities of A Leader* by John C. Maxwell, *The Purpose Driven Life* by Rick Warren, and *Live Your Best Life Now* by Joel Osteen. All are great sources of motivation.

If I read something that I find very enlightening, I write it down on a note card, carry it around in my pocket, and read over it often until it becomes an affirmation. I suggest you find or write several affirmations that you can say to yourself when you are in doubt. Affirmations are positive statements that affirm a state of being. When I feel myself getting the impulse to pick up the phone and make the wrong call, a call that could be dialing pain, I say to myself over and over again, "As a Man among Men I am Faithful and True." Then, as I begin to really listen to those words and believe them, I see how powerfully they impact my life in a healthy way.

Chapter 4
Don't Do What He Did

"I looked for a man among them who would build up the wall and stand before me in the gap on behalf of the land so I would not have to destroy it, but I found none." -Ezekiel 22:30 (NIV)

When I was young I had two heroes: Earvin "Magic" Johnson and my dad. It seems like only yesterday that Magic announced his first retirement from the NBA due to his HIV infection. It is a vivid image in my mind, although it happened more than fifteen years ago, on November 7, 1991, to be exact. I watched the live news conference on television, and then I lay down on the floor of our living room and cried. I cried so hard I could barely make out the blurred picture on the TV screen because of my tears. I told my mom he would be dead in ten years. I wasn't mad, but I was disappointed. My heart ached. I still liked Magic, but he was no longer a hero. My dad and my great-grandfather were the only two men I looked up to from then on.

Daddy was a welder and he worked at a huge plant in Rockdale, a small town thirty miles north of Giddings. He had worked there for eleven years when he was unexpectedly laid off. On the day Daddy lost his job, he stopped by my mom's house to visit my older brother and me. As he told us about the layoff, he was visibly sad and angry. I didn't know it at the time, but my dad had a drinking problem. I had seen him drink when he was with me and I had even seen him drink beer while he was driving. I didn't think it was a big deal. Whenever I heard people talking about not drinking and driving, I didn't think it was that important. I honestly believed that don't drink and drive meant just that—don't drink while driving. After Daddy left from visiting with my brother and me, he drove to a bar and got drunk. Later, while driving home he took a curve too fast and had a serious accident, flipping his truck into a ditch and rolling into a fence. Thank God the accident happened in front of a house and the man who lived there was awakened by the noise. The gentleman called 911 and then rushed out of his house to help Daddy. The man happened to be someone who knew my great-grandfather and had met Daddy a few times. Daddy went to the hospital with injuries but they were not life-threatening. The next morning, my mom told my brother and me about the accident. It finally clicked—at that moment I figured out what was meant by "don't drink and drive." After the accident, Daddy decided to stop drinking. He started going to Alcoholics Anonymous and he has been sober for over twenty years. Daddy shared with me, several years after the accident, that he realized his family was more important to him than alcohol. He also realized that if he didn't make a change, he would end up either in jail or dead, and he didn't want to sacrifice his life for alcohol. So he decided to get sober and stay sober.

Daddy didn't know it at the time but being laid off gave him a great opportunity to pursue more in life than just being a welder. Napoleon Hill wrote, "When the opportunity came, it appeared in a different form and from a different direction than…expected. That is one of the tricks of opportunity. It has a sly habit of slipping in by the back door, and often it comes disguised in the form of misfortune, or temporary defeat. Perhaps this is why so many fail to recognize opportunity." Eventually,

Daddy went back to school and became a certified mechanical engineer inspector. He was hired by a very large firm in Chicago and, because Daddy had been a welder for over eleven years before he became a mechanical engineer inspector, he was an asset in more ways than one. With Daddy's new opportunity he was able to work from his home until he was called to go to a plant to conduct a formal inspection. Being called to do a formal inspection meant traveling to almost any place in the world— Africa, Thailand, Kuwait, China, Canada. You name it and Daddy has more than likely been there once or twice. The same goes for his travels in the states.

As a youngster, I had a special relationship with my daddy. I was his baby boy and proud of it. I remember how no matter where he was in the world he very rarely missed a sporting event that I was participating in. I would be warming up on the court before my basketball game and when I looked up, Daddy was there, standing by the bleachers. I would be on the football field stretching and when I looked up, there was Daddy standing right by the uprights, talking with Coach. I remember the first time I scored a touchdown. It happened while I was in middle school. Daddy gave me five dollars and said that for every touchdown I scored he would give me an additional five bucks. Luckily for him, I didn't score too many more touchdowns.

Also, I was extremely blessed to have been raised by my Papa, my great-grandfather, who used to tell me, "You can have all of the book sense in the world but if you don't have any common sense then the book sense really doesn't matter because you are still lost." I learned some valuable lessons when I was twelve years old about how fear and peer pressure can steal the power of being true to myself, and how good old common sense can help me avoid situations that have the potential for landing me in a lot of trouble. When I was twelve I almost drowned. Now, as far as

I can remember, it seems like Dywarne, who is four years older than me, had always known how to swim. We spent our summers with our great-grandparents on their farm. One day during the summer that I was twelve, my great-grandfather and his nephew, Bo Duke, were visiting with some relatives near a tank. There were some kids swimming in the tank and Dywarne went to join them, so I tagged along. When we reached the tank it seemed to me to be a magical place. Kids were swinging on tires that had been tied to ropes hanging from trees. The kids would swing high in the air and then jump from the tire, splashing into the water. It looked like something you would see in a Country Time lemonade commercial. People were also diving from the trees into the tank. They all were having so much fun. Dywarne immediately jumped in and begin to play also. Soon the other kids began asking me to jump in. I told them I didn't know how to swim and they started teasing me. I became afraid that my big brother and the other kids would think I wasn't cool if I didn't jump in. I began to feel the peer pressure that came from being the only kid standing at the edge of the water. Finally, any commitment I had to being true to myself just slipped away and into the water I jumped, and I almost died! Suddenly remembering that I didn't know how to swim, I began to fight against the water. Dywarne and another kid helped me to the edge of the tank. I caught my breath and got out of the water.

We didn't know it at the time, but Bo had eased his way down to the tank to see what my older brother and I were doing. As soon as he saw me jump into the tank, he ran back to tell our great-grandfather (Bo called him Uncle Buddy). I can still hear him now, "Uncle Buddy, Uncle Buddy, Dywarne and J. are down in that tank with those other boys and, you know, J. doesn't know how to swim!" After getting his report from Bo, we could hear Papa calling for us in the distance. Soaked to the bone, we ran back up the hill and through the pasture to where Papa was standing near the driver's side of his truck. He had tears in his eyes. My Papa was a firm man when he needed to be, but even more so he was a very tenderhearted man who could cry in a heartbeat. He was not a tall man, maybe around five feet six inches, and his personality reminded me a lot of the character Augustus "Gus" McCrae, played by Robert Duvall, in the movie *Lonesome Dove*. When it was time to take care of business, you could count on him and, more than anything else, Papa was adventurous, sincere and expressed raw, heartfelt emotions.

Papa knew that a tank was manmade and the depth of the water was unpredictable. For your first few steps you would be wading in shallow water and then, suddenly, because of a ten-foot drop off, you would be fighting to keep your head above water. I looked over his shoulder and saw Bo standing on the other side of the truck with a little smirk on his face. Papa said, "I'm going to give you both a whipping and I'll tell you why. Dywarne, you are the oldest and you are supposed to be your brother's keeper and you know that J. doesn't know how to swim. J., you shouldn't do what you see everyone else doing even if they are family. And if either one of you had drowned, your mom and dad would have killed me." That said, he walked over to the truck, opened the driver's door, and pulled an eight-foot bull whip from behind the seat. I had a track record for running when it was time for me to get a well-deserved whipping but on that day I could barely move. Papa told my brother and me to stand side by side with our hands placed on the hood of the truck. Then he told Bo to hold our hands down. Papa gave us both three licks at the same time and with each one we yelled at the top of our lungs from the unimaginable pain. When he finished, Papa was crying more than Dywarne and I were. Even Bo was crying. Papa hugged us both and continued to cry, telling us how much he loved us. That was the first and only time Papa ever whipped me and it was the best whipping I ever had in my life. I'm not saying that's what people need to do to their kids, but it sure worked for me.

Over the years I have remembered the lessons I learned about fear, peer pressure and being true to myself. When Dywarne began to make poor decisions and get involved with drugs, I remembered what Papa told me and I said to myself, don't do what he did. When I was in college and one of the guys I used to hang out with stopped showing up for class, I remembered what my Papa told me and I said to myself, don't do what he did. In some cases I have tested those lessons to see if I was bigger or bolder, but deep down in my gut I've known when to tell myself, don't do what he did.

When my parents divorced, my daddy, unlike most men, stuck around and was involved with every aspect of my life from childhood, through college, and still to this day. Daddy didn't believe in paying child support. Not because he didn't want to support his children, but because he didn't want to support someone else's household. The State of Texas didn't see it that way, yet instead of giving my mother child support so she could give Dywarne and me what we needed, Daddy would just give us whatever we needed himself. For example, if we needed back-to-school clothes, Daddy would buy us back-to-school clothes. When I was young, I could only see the situation from my daddy's point of view, mainly, I think, because he didn't live with us. I now believe that deep down I was scared I might lose his love and affection if I didn't always agree with his actions or with the often less than kind words he used when telling Dywarne and me how he felt about my mama.

He probably won't admit it but I feel that there is a part of my dad that loves my mom deeply. He knows that because of his drinking, his arrogance and pride, or maybe because they were too young to be married, their marriage didn't last. There is a part of him that he hasn't fully forgiven and it pisses him off sometimes when he thinks about how it could have been. I know because he's always asking me questions like "Did you tell your mama?" and "What did Kathy think?" and the tone in his voice seems to be seeking some kind of approval, almost as if he is reminding me that he is different now. When I was younger I was always quick to mouth off to my friends, telling them that I didn't have a memory of my parents being married because they divorced when I was around two years old. I would say this in a matter-of-fact tone of voice to show them that it didn't bother me and I had made it just fine. I never talked much about my parents' divorce, mostly because I was too young to remember it, but it hurt. It left a wound.

Dad was present and active as best as he could be in the lives of Dywarne and me, but nevertheless, I still had a hurtful wound inside of me. Dr. Robert Lewis, founder of the Men's Fraternity at Fellowship Bible Church in Little Rock, Arkansas, refers to this as "the absent father wound." He defines it as an ongoing emotional, social, or spiritual deficit ordinarily not found in a healthy relationship with one's dad that must now be overcome by other means. I know that my dad wasn't absent in my life, but maybe because of the divorce, I felt something was missing. Dr. Lewis goes on to say that the results of the absent father wound could show up as pain and anger, extreme behaviors such as addictions or obsessions, an inner sense of loneliness or incompleteness, or homosexuality.

I have only a handful of memories of daddy, Dywarne, and me sitting down at the dinner table and enjoying a good home-cooked meal—just the three of us. I feel the conversation that takes place around a dinner table, with the T.V. off, draws a family closer. When I think of the family I will have one day, I get excited about the moments we will share while eating a home-cooked meal together. That's one of those simple activities which strengthens the foundation of a family. While I was living with my mom, we often enjoyed dinner together at the table. Although my daddy, Dywarne, and I shared a meal at the dinner table only occasionally, each one was special because it was just us guys and we weren't doing it because it was a holiday, but because we *wanted* to be together!

Since Dad was such a ladies' man, I sometimes felt I was competing with the women in his life to win his attention. I thank God for my aunt Becky. I spent a lot of summers with her and also with my great-grandparents and grandmothers, but it still wasn't enough. I remember breaking down and crying in Aunt Becky's car one night as we drove back to her house. She was living on the north side of Houston and Dad was living on the south side. I wanted to see him but he was with some woman. My dad wasn't there for me and his absence left a hole. Dr. Lewis says the son will fill the hole with something that is a cheap and tragic substitute. I began to fill the hole with the first sexual images I saw in a hardcore adult magazine I found when my cousins, Dywarne and I were helping another aunt, my Aunt Judy, move. She had a black trash bag filled with old papers, books and magazines. I reached inside the bag and pulled out an image I have been trying to let go of ever since. That happened when I was about eight years old.

My mom remarried in 1984 and so I did have a male figure in our household. Unfortunately, the relationship was filled with turmoil. My dad would tell us that he wasn't going to have another man telling his two boys what to do and my stepdad would say he wasn't going to have another man telling him what to do in his own household. So in my early years, it was hard for me to form a tight relationship with my stepdad. From the beginning, my mom wanted me to call him "daddy" and that made me uncomfortable because I already had a daddy. And my dad always seemed pissed off at anything he heard about my stepdad. I know they both had their reasons, but I had a lot of anger, resentment, and pain around the entire situation. I didn't begin to have a real connection with my stepdad until I reached my late teenage years.

My mom and stepdad have been married for over twenty-four years. Their marriage hasn't been perfect but they are my inspiration when I think of a marriage that gets better with time. I sometimes think of them as Bill and Clara from the *Cosby Show*. I love my stepdad with all of my heart. He is a good man. We maybe didn't start off on the right foot, however, now we are dancing up a storm like there is no tomorrow and that's all that really matters.

As I look back, I can see how I have always felt a need to please my daddy and earn his love even if it might mean making Mom feel like I was taking sides. The year I was in eighth grade, a warrant was issued for my dad's arrest because he hadn't been making his child support payments. Daddy owed over $3000 in back child support. One Sunday evening he stopped by the house in Giddings to visit me. We didn't have a phone at the house so it was not unusual for my stepdad or my mom to walk across the street to Aunt Mamie's house and use her phone, so, as Dad and I stood outside talking beside his truck, neither of us thought it was a big deal when my step dad walked across the street to Aunt Mamie's house. Shortly thereafter, a cop car pulled up beside Daddy and the officer began to ask him questions. And right there in front of my eyes, I saw my hero put into handcuffs, escorted into the back seat of the police car, and taken off to jail. I ran into the house crying and yelling at my mom. I had never been as angry at Mama as I was that day.

Daddy had to go to court, and he asked if I would testify against Mom to help prove that when he did pay child support for Dywarne and me, Mom didn't use the money on us. Feeling like I needed to be loyal to Daddy and still holding on to my anger at my Mom, I agreed to testify. Buddha said, "Holding on to anger is like grasping a hot coal with the intent of throwing it at someone else; you are the one getting burned." When I walked into that courtroom to testify against my mom, I saw the sadness in her eyes when she looked up and saw me, and it made me want to crawl under a rock and die. I was told to go and wait in a little room until the Court called for me. Thank God, my name was never called. Later, Daddy told me that he had changed his mind. I think God changed Daddy's mind. Needless to say, Daddy did have to pay those three thousand dollars in back child support.

As I look back at those early years, I can see that Mom did an awesome job with what she had. There was a point in my childhood that she was between jobs, my stepdad was unemployed and we were living off food stamps. So when she would get a child support check in the mail, she would pay the light bill or the water bill, or buy food so that we could eat. My mom may not have always done what was right, in the eyes of my dad, and I can see why Daddy had reasons to be upset. But the law is the law even though sometimes it may not seem fair. Unfortunately, when children are exposed to a parent's anger, emotional wounds can cut real deep.

As we became young men, Daddy gave Dywarne and me the advice that fathers give their sons: don't do drugs, keep your nose clean, don't take any wooden nickels (in other words, don't be a fool), and, my favorite, if you wind up in jail, you better call your mother because if you call me, things will get even worse! With that in mind, I have always been cautious regarding alcohol and drugs. I have had my share of misfortunes, but in the back of my head I know Daddy is a recovering alcoholic so I've done my best to learn from his mistakes and not do what he did. Dywarne has been struggling with drugs since his teen years. I'm not a saint but drugs just didn't do it for me. Whatever I saw Dywarne do that was not pleasing to Daddy, I did just the opposite. I was more driven to keep Daddy proud of me by doing what I thought *he* would want me to do than by what I actually wanted to do. I've always felt a need to be bigger and better and make a lot of money probably because when Daddy was upset, it was usually about money. I often thought to myself, "Don't be like your father. Be better than him. Make him proud. Become a doctor." I prided myself on not having a problem with alcohol or an addiction to drugs.

As I matured, I learned more from Daddy's actions than from his words. About the time I began college, I became more aware of the fact that Daddy dated a *lot* of women, and more than one at a time. He definitely was a ladies' man. I figured that was the way to find the right woman. Daddy did it and since he was also a deacon in the church, it didn't seem like the worst thing in the world, as long as you didn't get busted. So why couldn't I do it? It wasn't uncommon. With the exception of the pastors I had known, most of the men I knew dated several women at the same time or were married with a "lady friend" on the side. Most of those men were shady when it came to the subject of relationships with women. It wasn't unusual for me to be asked by Pappa, Daddy, an uncle, or a male cousin how many women I was dating. An answer of anything under two just didn't seem good enough.

So as I entered my freshman year at Hardin-Simmons, I began dating a lot more and having sexual relationships with many different women. I thought that as long as I didn't get a sexually transmitted disease or get anyone pregnant, I wasn't hurting anyone. As I entered my senior year, my thoughts began to change. Daddy was on his third marriage and I was always dating a different woman. I may not have been causing any physical pain for anyone, but I was definitely causing a lot of emotional pain. I was also causing a lot of emotional and spiritual pain for myself. In fact, I realized I had developed a compulsive need to be with a woman instead of an honest desire.

People have many different places to choose from when they want to be in solitude and have a heart-to-heart with God. Some like to be in their "closet," whether it be literal or symbolic. Others prefer the outdoors, perhaps a park. For me, it's the shower. The shower is where I love to go and just let myself connect with God and pour my heart out. With the water as hot as possible, I like to get on my knees and let the water wash over my neck and back. I feel as if God is washing away my sins as I open myself up completely to Him.

I recall one night during my senior year when I was on my knees praying to God for a good woman. It was ironic because at that point in my life I was dogging every woman I dated, but there I was, praying for Him to bless me with a good woman. I asked God to bless me with a woman who was a Christian, intelligent, and beautiful, and one who had a great sense of humor. I prayed for a woman who would not stand behind me but beside me, a woman who wouldn't follow me into a pothole if I was headed that way, but who would have the foresight to step to the side and warn me, "Watch your step, babe, it's dangerous over there." I wanted a woman who would pick me up if I fell down while playing the game of life, a companion, a friend, a helpmate. I knew what I wanted and needed in a woman, but I continued to cheat on one woman after another.

Old habits die hard and years later after some serious

heartache from trying to will my relationships into what I thought God wanted, I began to look at the man in the mirror. Only when I started making sincere changes in my life and loving myself the way God loves me, did God bless me with such a woman in Saran. I am glad to say I finally have a woman who gives me what I need and want. She even gives me what I need when I may not want it! But, in those cases, God reminds me of the prayer I prayed on my knees during my senior year in college, and deep down in my heart I know Saran is right. I know now that in a relationship, love means giving yourself—physically, mentally, emotionally, and spiritually—100 percent. You can't have a "lady friend" on the side. Before Saran, when I had a girlfriend whom I claimed I wanted to marry, I would still keep women on the side just in case I got upset with my girlfriend. Even if I wasn't having sex with my "lady friends," I was still emotionally cheating on my girlfriend because I was expressing my frustration regarding our relationship with my "lady friends" instead of with my girl friend. Don't try to rationalize your behavior if you have a woman on the side. If your girlfriend doesn't know about it and would not approve of it, then you've already made a mistake.

Yes, it is a risk when you give yourself completely to another person, and, yes, there is always a chance that you will be hurt when you allow yourself to be vulnerable. But, it's in the giving of you and in the allowing you to be vulnerable that a beautiful relationship is created—relinquishing control and surviving, instead, on trust and faith. There's the possibility the relationship may not work out and it may end, but you can't put a price on your own integrity, on being able to look in the eyes of the man in the mirror. Robert Bly speaks of this so well in his book, *Iron John*:

"That experience of being looked back at sobers us up immediately. If, as human beings, we have any doubts about the existence of the interior soul, we give up those doubts instantly.

When we look in the mirror, someone looks back questioning, serious, alert, and without intent to comfort; and we feel more depth in the eyes looking at us than we ordinarily sense in our own eyes as we stare out at the world. How strange! Who could it be that is looking at us? We conclude that it is another part of us, the half that we don't allow to pass out of our eyes when we glance at others—and that darker and more serious half looks back at us only at rare times. Antonio Machado said:

Look for your other half
who walks always next to you
and tends to be who you aren't.
Translated by R. B.

"The person who gazes in the mirror receives an awareness of his other half, his shadow, or hidden man; awareness of that hidden man is a proper aim for all initiation. The experience teaches him that the eyes he sees are not just 'him,' but some other man, not included very well under the name his parents gave him, Edward or Lance or Kerry. These eyes belong to some other being whom we have never met. Juan Ramon Jimenez said:

I am not I.
I am this one
Walking beside me, whom I do not see,
Whom at times I manage to visit,
And at other times I forget.
The one who forgives, sweet, when I hate,
The one who remains silent when I talk,
The one who takes a walk when I am indoors,
The one who will remain standing when I die.
Translated by R.B.

"The one we see in the mirror is complicated, and the glance that takes one moment in the tale could take several years in life. The one looking back is at the same time a man's shadow, or dark side, and also his spiritual twin, his white shadow. Rolf Jacobsen, the Norwegian poet, calls him

your shadow, the white one,
whom you cannot accept,
and who will never forget you.
Translated by R.B."

You are not weak when you choose to live a life of honesty, accountability, and integrity with your woman. You are actually very strong. If you haven't noticed, the trend in today's society is to be unfaithful, but not get caught. As the old saying goes, "If it was easy, then everybody would be doing it." It isn't easy, but if an honest and pure relationship is your heart's desire, there comes a point when, men, you must make a change and stop being whoremongers. It's written in the Bible, James 1:23-25: "Anyone who does not do what it says is like a man who looks at his face in a mirror and, after looking at himself, goes away and immediately forgets what he looks like. But the man who looks intently into the perfect law that gives freedom, and continues to do this, not forgetting what he has heard, but doing it, he will be blessed in what he does."

A friend of mine named Michael Newhouse once said, "How a person spends his day is how he will live his life." Many people spend their days living out their shadows. By that I mean living in secrecy, living out of integrity and not being accountable, or procrastinating. For many men, their shadow side includes being unfaithful to their wives, spending their time with "lady friends." We all have a shadow side. The important thing here is not what the shadow is but noticing how we react to it. When we hide from it, deny it or feel hopeless about our behavior, our shadow side controls us and we keep repeating the behavior. Days become months which become years, and how we spend each day becomes how we live our lives. If we want our lives to change, we need to introduce some light to our shadow. By light I mean self-understanding, compassion for ourselves and time spent getting to know our shadow. Once we bring the shadow into the light, we can release it and we no longer need to hide, deny or feel hopeless.

After looking at my shadows, I knew it was time for me to make a change. While I was trying to run from developing the addictions my dad and older brother had, I was actually running full speed ahead into my own addiction. As it has often been said, "What you run from is what you end up becoming unless you choose to face the fear head on." I realized I had to make a choice: If I chose to avoid who I really was, going in the opposite direction of the man I was, I knew I would live an unfulfilled life. I also knew there wasn't enough money, women, titles, or material objects to fill the void I would feel. No matter how often I went to church or how much I tithed, I would always be a man filled with anger, rage and fury. I had seen this pattern in the lives of my grandfather and my father. I recognized it because I had created the same pattern in my own life. Their lives reflected back to me the truth of my own. I am no better or worse but equal. What a gift! Instead of judging them for their mistakes, I was able to love them for helping me see my mistakes more clearly.

I can empathize with my older brother because, like him, I too have the ability to feel powerless and passive—too powerless to try and fail, and passive enough to settle for just getting by. As he continues to try and make the right choices to live a life of sobriety, I see in his eyes the brilliant man we are both capable of becoming. Thus, he inspires me to be like the Samurai warrior who before going into battle meditates on his fear, embraces it and then pictures

it sitting on the very tip of his sword, and later drives that fear into and through his enemy.

In October of 2003 I was living with my dad. It was weird because I had lived the previous five years on my own and, now, to be waiting tables and living with my dad when I had a college degree just didn't make sense. And to make things worse, my dad was acting like he still thought I was ten or eleven. He constantly wanted to know what I was doing, who was I talking to on the phone, when had I met that person, and so on and so on. I guess my dad still thought I was a child, and I felt I was transitioning into manhood. In my mind's eye I could see my Big Mama shaking her head and saying "two grown men under one roof." My hero, my dad.

One Thursday night I came home from working a double shift at the restaurant, feeling like I was beginning to get sick. Back when I was in college, whenever I felt a cold coming on, I would buy a gallon of orange juice and just drink that for the next couple of days. Well, that evening when I came in, my dad and stepmom weren't around so I put a note on the orange juice container that said "Please don't drink. I am sick." I had learned very quickly in college that if you don't want something of yours eaten or drunk by someone else, you really need to leave a note on it.

It is not often that we get the opportunity to see the passing of the torch. For example, when an athlete gets the chance to play his hero—Magic Johnson against Doctor J or Kobe Bryant against Michael Jordan—it's the passing of the torch, a moment in which everything he has been working for comes together. He has an opportunity to both pay homage to and play against the person he has admired (and probably still pretends to be).

My hero, my father. My hero was my father and there had been many times throughout my life when I had tried to imitate him. He was my standard by which I had measured myself. But how do you go from the excitement of playing against your hero to the pain of fighting him? I felt hurt when I fought my hero…I felt broken. It all started later that Thursday night when my hero, my father, asked me why I had written that note on the orange juice container. I told him I did it because I was sick and had come in late after working a double and since no one else was home at the moment, I left a note so no one would drink the juice. My hero felt that I was being selfish and he reminded me of all the time he had spent visiting me while I was in college, all the hours driving down the highway, having to pull over to the side of the road to get some sleep, and all the money he had spent taking care of me and buying me stuff throughout my entire life. And my hero complained about how my mama never had anything to give me and that she never had any money. And my hero ranted on about how he didn't have to stay around and how he could have been like most men and left me to fend for myself, but he hadn't done that.

All my life I had listened to this ranting and raving. It happened whenever my dad felt he wasn't getting the praise he deserved for sticking around, or when he felt he was owed something. On that particular night, I was tired of feeling guilty about all he had done for me and I was tired of being constantly reminded that my mom was worthless and of feeling like I owed my entire existence to him. So as I stormed upstairs, I yelled out loud that this is bullshit!!! That was all it took to set a blaze to the rage in my hero. I admitted I was wrong for what I said. But all of the yelling and cussing that followed, hmmm, yeah, it was pretty bad. I never touched my hero but he touched me. He tried to provoke me into taking a swing at him but I didn't. I could tell he wanted me to fight so that he could justify his behavior, rationalize his way of thinking, and so he could say he was trying to protect himself or that I gave him no choice but to fight back.

It is written in Ephesians 6:4 "And, ye fathers, provoke not your children to wrath; but bring them up in the nurture and admonition of the Lord." I never touched him, even though my hero touched me, pushed me, yelled at me and cussed, trying his hardest to get me to come to blows with him. I never would, I never did, but I did fight, not with a punch but with the words that came out of my mouth, yelling that I would never treat my son the way you are treating me right now, with body language, and with anger-filled tears that rolled down my face. I choked on my tears. I hurt because the relationship with the man I had looked up to for years had come to this: My hero fought me and I fought back. Paradoxically, the words that came to mind at that point and which have helped me heal were words my dad had shared with me when I was much younger. He had said, "Don't put all your faith in humans because they will sometimes let you down, maybe not intentionally, but just because they are human beings. Someone may say that he is going to pick you up the next morning at eight and he wakes up to a flat tire." Simple words but still full of wisdom.

My dad is no longer my hero. I look up to my dad and I love him. I respect him. I honor him. I still think he is a great man. I now think of him as an imperfectly perfect man. My hero is God, and only God. I know He is with me now and will be until the end of the world and beyond. He will never leave me nor forsake me. Others have betrayed me, made me fearful, hurt me and wounded me but I know God will never treat me that way. God is my ultimate Father and I am His ultimate son.

Then, older and wiser, I discovered I had more admiration for Magic Johnson than I ever dreamed possible. I admired him for being an amazing businessman and entrepreneur rather than an outstanding basketball player. Not too many athletes could leave the game the way he did and transcend to where they were able

71

to make a bigger impact on society than they did as athletes on the basketball court. He could have hung up the towel, content with being one of the greatest basketball players to ever play the game. In some ways I aspired to be like him as a businessman because I believed he didn't want people just to be good, but to be their best at what they did. As I came full circle in my thoughts, I saw Magic as a role model. He exemplified an act of metamorphosis because he changed and adapted in order to live his life to the fullest instead of becoming stagnant and dying. I express that same sentiment for my dad.

However, because of those occasions where we haven't seen things eye to eye, and because our communication had become strained in recent years, I made an effort to reach out to my dad. My dad didn't always know what I needed from him. I realized that my dad couldn't know what I needed unless I told him. There are many people today who are in relationships or situations where they are unhappy, but they continue to follow the same path because they have not made an effort to tell the other person what they need. There is a difference between sharing with a person what it is you need and them not responding or not being receptive, and not expressing yourself at all. I knew I had to share my feelings, no matter how my dad might respond.

What I needed from my dad was a different form of love. Until I read *The Five Love Languages* by Gary Chapman, which was recommended to me by Michael Smith (a sincere friend), I didn't know that love *was* a language. Gary Chapman believes there are five love languages: words of affirmation, quality time, receiving gifts, acts of service, and physical touch. At different stages in my life, Daddy had given me each of those forms of love. The language of love Daddy expressed the most was acts of service. As I was growing up he would tell me, "Son, when you get in the position to begin taking care of yourself, then you will be a big help to Daddy. Being able to provide for J. is enough for me." Well, the more I became able to provide for J., the more distant Daddy and I became. Daddy felt he wasn't needed if I wasn't asking for something, especially money. It wasn't that I didn't need him anymore. I had grown into an adult who was using what my dad, my mom and others had taught me—to stand on my own two feet and live life without looking for someone to bail me out when life got hard. With Daddy being unable to give me acts of service, our conversations became less frequent until we got to the point where we were talking only once a month, if not less. I knew exactly which one of Chapman's five love languages I needed from my dad. What I needed, more than anything else, was "quality time."

Mr. Chapman wrote that "quality time" means giving someone your undivided attention. When you give someone twenty minutes of your undivided attention and that person reciprocates, you are giving each other twenty minutes of life. He further wrote that a central aspect of quality time is "togetherness," not proximity. Two people sitting in the same room are in close proximity, but they are not necessarily together. Togetherness has to do with focused attention. It means they are doing something together and they are giving their full attention to each other. The important thing is that they are spending focused time with each other. Mr. Chapman also writes that another aspect of quality time is a "quality conversation." A quality conversation is a sympathetic dialogue where two individuals are sharing their experiences, thoughts, feelings and desires in a friendly, uninterrupted context. Each person is listening sympathetically to what is said by the other and then asking questions, not in a badgering manner, but with a genuine desire to understand the other person's thoughts, feelings, and desires.

Daddy can be real stubborn and I can be the exact same way, so I knew that if I wanted our relationship to grow and not remain stagnant, I was going to have to make the first move. I shared with Daddy that I felt we had drifted apart and he shared that he felt the same. I told him about the five love languages and I told him that what I needed from him was quality time. All I wanted was to just speak with him on the phone, to call one another and talk. I didn't want him to be thinking, "I shouldn't have to call him because I'm his dad and he should call me," and I wanted to stop thinking, "I am not going to call Daddy because he is my dad and he should call me." I wanted us to just pick up the phone and call. It didn't have to matter who called who first. I just wanted one of us make the call, and I wanted there to be an open line of quality communication between us. I let him know I still needed him and his love—I just happened to be at a point in my life where I needed his love in a different language. Once I made this known to him he was enlightened and we have been growing closer in a different form of love. If I hadn't said anything, we both would have continued on with the same old pattern, not moving closer but further apart.

My love for my dad has grown deeper because I know him now to be a man who stuck by his family. Realizing he had an addiction to alcohol and not wanting that addiction to disconnect him from his two boys, he made a sacrifice that most people are not willing to make. Most people are not willing to say, "Hey, if I don't change, my alcoholism is going to cause me to be thrown in jail or out on the streets, or, much worse, to kill myself or someone else. Then I won't be able to have a positive influence on my children's lives." Most people are not willing to say, "I need to get help! I need to change!" Daddy was honest enough with himself to realize this and to get the help he needed. It was not easy. It was the most difficult decision he had to make in his life. Since the day he made that choice, he has been sober one day at a time.

Making difficult choices, such as the one my dad made, brings up feelings of fear—a normal response all people experience. But when it happens, we need to look fear right in the eye and step forward. When we get to a point, and we will, where we can look back and see the situation we have come through, we realize that by facing our fear and going through it, we are now a better and more enlightened person. We have expanded our horizons and stepped outside of our comfort zone. I faced those hair-raising moments, especially when getting help for my sex addiction. And now I look back and say, "Jonathan, why did you wait so long? Why did you hesitate? Look how good and positive you feel now." I have not always felt that way, but I now know it was all according to God's timing as to when I decided to step into that fear. When I stopped wanting to control my life and I trusted that God had complete control over my life, I was finally able to make the decision to embrace my fears.

In April 2006, I joined the Mankind Project. In our mission statement we declare that "we are an order of men called to reclaim the sacred masculine for our time through initiation, training, and action in the world." We seek to change the world one man at a time. All men are initiated into the organization through an experiential, educational weekend called "The New Warrior Training Adventure." Then they spend a couple of hours each week checking in with members of small "integration" groups intended to offer support and accountability. Like a stone dropping into a pond, the New Warrior Training sends ripples through the lives of men, their families, and their communities. Unlike one-day, self-help workshops, the Mankind Project continues long after the sentinel weekend event. This international organization has thirty-eight centers where more than 30,000 men have been initiated since 1985. The more I looked at the man in the mirror, the more I came to grips with the truth—I needed to love and honor all of me. Not just my good characteristics but also the parts of myself I strive to shed. The Mankind Project has helped me live my life with more integrity, accountability, authenticity, and focus. The result: feeling more connected to the present moment. It has helped me step into my fear and embrace my power. I pass stories about my experiences on to anyone who will listen!

In April 2007, my father joined the Mankind Project. I am so proud of my dad. The little boy in me invited him to the warrior weekend to see the man I have become. He helped birth an imperfectly perfect son. I feel after seeing Dad do his warrior weekend that I have birthed an imperfectly perfect father. This reconnection with Dad is one of the greatest feelings I have ever felt in my life. It feels so pure and supernatural that I know it could only come from God. The relationship we have has opened my eyes to the true meaning of God's unconditional love. When I looked into my dad's eyes during the goodbye ceremony, it was the first time I can remember looking at him and seeing not just my dad, but a man. He was a man before he became my father, a man with his own dreams, hopes, struggles, pain, and love. Yes, he is a father but I have had to learn over time that he also is a human being. Life's deepest meaning is not found in accomplishments but in relationships. The relationship I have with my dad, in my judgment, is the greatest it's ever been and every day it continues to climb to higher and higher levels of love.

Dr. Robert Lewis, founder of The Men's Fraternity—The Quest for Authentic Manhood, wrote that every son wants and needs from his father time together, life skills, direction with solid "why" answers, conviction through modeling (you will leave in your son what you've lived out in your home), and his dad's heart, for example, I love you, son, I am proud of you, and you are good at (whatever that may be). Proverbs 17:6 says, "Children's children are the crown of old men; and the glory of children are their fathers."

As I consider everything I have accomplished in my life, all the awards, honors, and praise, and everything I might accomplish in the future, I am convinced that the greatest gift I have ever received and will ever receive was given to me on October 14, 2007. My dad and I had just finished a New Warrior Training Adventure weekend together. He was on his way back to his home in Hockley, Texas, feeling dog tired, and I was driving back to my home in Dallas, completely exhausted and barely able to keep my eyes open. My dad called me and he said, "Son, have you got a sec? I just wanted to tell you that I am proud of you. You have become a fine young man. Son, you encourage, inspire and motivate me to continue to become a better man. You are a great speaker. Stay grounded and approachable." That was the greatest moment of my life. I felt complete. I felt my dad's heart. I felt love and acceptance, and I was humbled. I will always remember those words.

All in all, my feelings toward my dad and my stepdad are best described by David Blankenhorn in his book, *Fatherless America*: "As a father, the good family man is not perfect, but he is good enough to be irreplaceable. He is a father on the premises. His children need him and he strives to give them what they need every day. He knows that nothing can substitute for him— nothing. Either he is a father, or his children are fatherless. He would never consider himself 'not that important.'" Lucky for me, I had two of them.

A man once asked me: "What can you at twenty-six teach me that I don't already know at forty-eight?" I told him that the answer to his question is something that he doesn't know.

Wisdom doesn't have an age. Wisdom is when you have learned so much from the mistakes you have made that you want to make them over again, and wisdom is the blessing you receive when you share those experiences with others. I told him that when that little voice inside of your soul says do it, you need to move, NOW! Move because when you look back it will have been worth it. You will have grown and learned something. You will have taken a problem and turned it into an opportunity for tomorrow's success.

Stan Goss said, "Men cry because life is beautiful but it is short." I invite you to consider that.

Chapter 5
A New Direction

"Behold, I am doing a new thing! Now it springs forth; do you not perceive and know it and will you not give heed to it? I will even make a way in the wilderness and rivers in the desert." - Isaiah 43:19(AMP)

In the summer of 1998, I left my hometown of Giddings, Texas, and moved on to Abilene, Texas, where I attended college. I actually began college a month early, in July instead of August, because I had scored a 19 on my ACT test and the university wanted to determine if I was capable of handling a college course load. This hesitancy on the part of the university was not a surprise to me, considering in high school I had taken the writing section of the TAAS test twice, the reading section twice, and the math section six times before finally passing and graduating with my classmates. Needless to say, I had struggled with test taking throughout my school years, but I was soon to discover that there was more beneath the surface than being a poor test taker.

So, during summer school I took six hours and passed, allowing me to officially enter Hardin-Simmons University as a freshman. I began college with high hopes of becoming a massage therapist so that I could massage beautiful women and make lots of money. My advisor quickly let me know that a degree in massage therapy was not offered at HSU!

My dad once told me that I was going to have to work for anything that was worthwhile. If I got it easy, it would not last long. With that in mind, I majored in biology and minored in psychology with plans to become a physical therapist. A small voice inside of me said, "A physical therapist? Never! How did you even come up with such an idea?" I told that small voice to shut up and I told myself that physical therapy was just like massage therapy but with more detail. I was off and running. I knew how I was going to make my fortune in the world. Now I just needed to tell enough people and hopefully in return I would begin to believe the lie that I was telling myself.

I was four and a half long hours away from home and not at all sure about what I wanted to do with my life, but I was living it as if I had all the answers. As I began to experience college life and all it offered, the answers gradually became more real.

I was on the varsity football team—at the time, we were the best team in NCAA division three football. We were always moving back and forth between the number one and number two poll positions. I played tight end. I wasn't a starter and I never really played much, but to me that didn't matter. I enjoyed encouraging both the guys on the field and my other teammates. I found happiness in motivating my teammates. To me, winning was important and a winning attitude had no room for false pride, over-inflated egos, and selfishness. I wanted to be a starter and I wanted to play, but if someone was better than me on Saturday morning then that's who needed to play so we could win.

In the spring of my freshman year I was still trying to persuade myself that I wanted to be a physical therapist. I had recently taken a biology exam and had earned a perfect score, but I was struggling to bring up my overall grade for the semester. My biology professor, Dr. Allan Landwer, called me to his office to discuss my goals and interests in medicine. Dr. Landwer had graduated from Texas Christian University with a masters in biology and his specialty was ecology. (He currently has a Ph.D. in biology and is a professor, a curator and the head of the biology department at Hardin-Simmons.) He spent most of his summers in Australia or Jamaica studying rare reptiles, particularly lizards. I respected Dr. Landwer and valued his opinion. He had a way of getting his point across and keeping it simple during the process. He asked me point blank why I wanted to become a physical therapist. I couldn't give him an answer. Then he broke it down like this: he told me that he had been observing me on campus and that I had a special gift—the ability to communicate with people in such a way that they felt absolutely comfortable in my presence, so comfortable, in fact, that they felt safe sharing personal information with me. This even included people like the university president, Dr. Craig Tuner, and the facilities coordinator, Mr. Tim McCarry. Then he asked me if I had ever considered becoming a doctor. He felt my gift should be shared with patients. I told him I had thought about becoming a doctor, but I didn't know what direction I needed to go in to become one. We ended the conversation with him telling me to just think about it and if I wanted to change my major, my advisor would be able to help me. As I left his office I recalled some words of wisdom my great-grandmother had shared with me when I was a child, "When you think someone is not looking, they are." That may be a good thing or a bad thing, depending on the situation. In this case it was a good thing. I was honored by the way Dr. Landwer viewed me.

People are funny. Throughout my entire life my parents, grandparents, family and friends have told me that I have the talent to do whatever it is that I want to do in life. Most of the time I just let their words roll off my shoulders. But now, when one person outside of my support group tells me the same exact thing that everyone else has been telling me for as long as I can remember, only now do I think it's true and I have hope! Up until this point, most of what I did in life (sports, college, sex, etc.) I did because I felt it was what people expected from me. So, was being a doctor my purpose in life? I needed to go somewhere to think and decide what direction I was going to go with my major.

I went to my barber shop. Not to get answers, but to relax. The owner of the shop and its only barber was Mrs. Lena Mae Jones. She was a kind and compassionate woman with a grand sense of humor. She reminded me of my grandmother, very active and full of wisdom. I would go the shop, not only because I needed a haircut, but to relax because the conversation at the shop was always positive. Everything was fair game—religion, sports, politics, current affairs, anything you wanted to talk about. You name it and it was discussed at Mrs. Lena Mae Jones's barber shop. Unfortunately, I was not in the mood to talk on this particular day because I was too busy replaying in my mind the conversation I had earlier with Dr. Landwer.

The gentleman in the chair, Mr. Tom Wall, who was getting his hair cut before me, didn't notice my state of mind. He was talking up a storm. But Mrs. Jones could sense that I was acting out of character and finally she told Mr. Wall to shut up. She asked me what was wrong and I told her I was thinking about changing my major to pre-med. Mr. Wall sat up in the barber chair and introduced himself. He informed me that if I was considering pre-med he could help me. Mr. Wall was a recently retired orthopedic nurse. We exchanged phone numbers and he told me that one of the doctors he used to work for would be giving me a call.

Later that day I received a phone call from Dr. Price Brock and the next morning I was in his office telling him about my sudden interest in medicine. Dr. Brock was a sports orthopedic surgeon but had retired from actually doing surgery. He was now referring patients to one of his four partners, Dr. Dale Funk, Dr. Paul McDonough, Dr. Robert Dickey, and Dr. Andrew Stoebner. Their clinic, Orthopedic Associates, was one of the premier orthopedic practices in the Taylor County area. I felt as if I was on top of the world. Here I was in the clinic talking with Dr. Brock and less than twenty-four hours had passed since I was just halfway thinking about becoming a doctor while speaking with Dr. Landwer.

I thought to myself, God sure does answer prayers, and fast, too. But, in all honesty, God had not answered my prayers because I had never prayed to God and shared with Him the thoughts I had and the fears I felt about going pre-med. As I think back over the decision I made in Dr. Brock's office to become a doctor, I realize I made it very selfishly. *I* made it. My spiritual priorities were not in the correct order when I decided that I wanted to become a doctor. I said "Bless it, Lord" like I was a puppet master or something. I realize now, after the decision was made, that I should have prayed first, waited, and then taken action. Not take action and then pray to God that if it is His will, bless it. Why? Because God cannot be controlled! Neither can He be told what to do, because God is always in control. Nevertheless, that's life; making decisions, learning from your mistakes, and moving on. It just happened to take me a while to learn from this particular decision regarding pre-med. Like football coaches had told me my whole life, "I'd rather you make a mistake or a bad play going full speed and all out than just moving off of the ball at half speed," so *I* told myself I was going to be a doctor and I hit the ground running at full speed.

The following Monday I changed my major to psychology and my minor to biology, gunning for a bachelor of behavioral science and going pre-med. My schedule suddenly became very busy. On Monday mornings before class I would shadow Dr. Funk during his surgery rounds, mostly observing total knee and hip replacements. On Tuesday mornings before class I would shadow Dr. Brock as he met with his patients and again sometimes before afternoon football practice. On Wednesdays I would shadow Dr. Funk at the outpatient hospital, then attend morning classes, afternoon chemistry lab, and football practice, and finally I would wait tables at Cypress Street Station where I worked four nights a week. Thursdays I would shadow Dr. Brock in the morning as he made his rounds and Dr. Funk in the afternoon while he performed a few surgeries. Fridays were pretty much the same as Wednesdays.

During this high-speed schedule my grades were at an all-time low. I was unexpectedly but understandably put on academic probation. I quickly realized that if I didn't improve my grades, I would lose my financial aid and be forced to quit college because I couldn't afford to attend Hardin-Simmons on my own. So during the spring semester of my sophomore year, I studied with my back against the wall. It has been said that "you are who you are when you are under pressure." My dad once told me, "Don't give up because that is what the devil wants you to do." So I was not about to flunk out of college. To secure my stay at HSU, I adopted the attitude of Malcolm X—"by any means necessary!" My head football coach, Jimmie Keeling, was, above everything else, pro-education. So if anyone had a low grade point average, Coach Keeling required him to attend a tutorial class once a week until his grades improved. I was attending the class even before I was put on probation, but it wasn't enough because it was just a big study hall and most of the guys would just goof off. I quickly learned that no one was going to give me what I needed unless I asked for it. So I asked for a personal tutor for the subjects I was having the most trouble in, and I began studying like there was no tomorrow because if I didn't pass, there wasn't going to be one. I felt like I was in high school again, meeting with Sister Chandler after football practice and studying for the TAAS so that I could graduate.

I used all the resources I could to improve my GPA and improve it I did. Not by much, but just enough for me to keep my financial aid and continue trying to meet the requirements to enter medical school. I was concerned with why all my life I had had to spend double the time studying to measure up with the people in my classes. I knew above everything else that my grades did not represent me as a person. I knew I was smart. I didn't need a letter grade to tell me that, but I did need it to make it out of college. The following semester I began retaking the courses in which I had done poorly the first time I took them. If you were to ask my friends what they felt my GPA was, they would have told you a 3.5, if not better, because I was always studying, there on the third floor of the library. I would never tell them what I made on an exam. I would just look at the grade on the first page of the exam and smile. They figured the smile meant J.O. had done pretty well. They took my smile to mean that I had earned a high B or, even better, an A. They never knew how hard I struggled.

Honestly, a smile was all I could muster up to cover the embarrassment and shame of failing another exam. In the eyes of my friends and most other people, I was intelligent. In reality, I wasn't smart on paper. I began to lie about my grades when anyone asked how I was doing. I just smiled my ass off and wove another beautiful mask of lies across my face. I was afraid that if I told my friends I had studied for an exam for over two weeks and then bombed it, they would think I was stupid and they wouldn't like me anymore. Why is it that once we become friends with another person, we feel a need to become something that we aren't to keep their friendship? Actually, in the long run, we usually end up losing our new friend because the friend no longer likes the person we have become.

A thought to ponder: *Do you know you?* I asked myself this question as I pondered over why I was studying like a madman and making grades like a reject (well, not all of my grades were bad but there were enough bad ones for me to be concerned).

During my junior year I was taking genetics for the second time when the instructor, Dr. Flanagan, told me she wanted to speak with me after class concerning our first exam. This was not the first time Dr. Flanagan was my instructor. I had failed genetics the first time I took it with her, so I wasn't too surprised when she asked to speak with me.

I had recently taken the first exam of the semester and I had been very frustrated because I knew so few answers. I had decided to flip the exam booklet over and on the back page I had written down all of the information we had covered up until that first exam. That was what Dr. Flanagan wanted to talk about. Dr. Flanagan told me that after looking at the back of the exam, she realized I had written down almost all of the information I needed to answer the questions correctly. She wanted to know why I hadn't used that information to answer the exam questions. I told her I didn't understand the questions on the exam and I felt pressured because everyone was finishing before me. I told her I didn't know how to take good notes which I could have used to study for the exam. So when I was studying on my own for the test, most of the information seemed new to me instead of being a review of what we had covered in class. It wasn't just her class either; the same applied for my math courses and biology.

Now, I must tell you here that at the beginning of every semester the protocol for each class is covered on the first day the class meets. And the instructor always mentions that if anyone feels they may have a learning disability, they should contact the person who is responsible for that department. In past years I hadn't paid attention to who was the director for students with learning disabilities, but after my rough start with a genetics class I was taking for the second time, I did a little research and discovered it was Mrs. Vicki Fehr. I knew Mrs. Fehr. I had taken a reading improvement course my freshmen year and she had been the instructor. I had earned a B for that course. Whenever Mrs. Fehr saw me on campus she would make a point to say hello and she would ask me to catch her up with what was going on in my life. I had always felt that Mrs. Fehr was someone with whom I could be vulnerable, but up to that point I had not been aware that she was responsible for helping students with learning disabilities.

After my talk with Dr. Flanagan, I felt it was time that I paid Mrs. Fehr a visit. I actually went by her office several times before knocking on the door, but I finally gave in when I reached the point where I was sick and tired of being sick and tired. I was tired of barely getting by and knowing deep down it wasn't because I didn't try. Once I finally knocked on her door, she greeted me with a smile that reassured me I was in the right place. We had a long talk during which I got her up to speed concerning my grades and my study habits. I also told her about the TAAS tests, the high school highs and lows, and everything else about my schooling as far back as I could remember. I expressed my concern to Mrs. Fehr that someone might find out I was talking to her. I was somewhat popular on campus and the last thing I wanted was for someone to find out that I might have a learning disability. In my mind that signaled weakness.

I have learned over time that once I bring my fear to the light it no longer has the power I gave it when I kept it in darkness. I feel more freedom when I acknowledge my fears. By expressing my vulnerability, I gain strength in knowing that whatever I feared is not as bad as it seemed when I kept it hidden in the shadows. I know that now, but I didn't know it back then.

Mrs. Fehr listened to everything I had to say. I was afraid she was going to judge me. Now I know people are going to judge me all my life. I can accept the criticism that applies to me and leave the rest behind. Some of it may be true but the rest is that other person's stuff, not mine.

Mrs. Fehr asked me to take a series of tests to help diagnose my disability. I agreed I should take the tests but I told her I couldn't afford them—the cost was around twelve hundred dollars. I wasn't going to ask my parents to help pay for them because I wanted everything to be confidential. I will remember what Mrs. Fehr did next for the rest of my life. She told me she wasn't going to charge me a single penny. God knows just when to send that person into your life that believes in you more than you believe in yourself. At that moment in my life, Mrs. Fehr was that person. She knew how serious I was about figuring out what was going on in my head and she was more than willing to go the distance to help me. For this I will forever be grateful to her.

After several weeks of me sneaking into Mrs. Fehr's office for testing, she finally told me I was dyslexic. I was immediately confused. My head was full of questions. I remember asking her what the word dyslexic meant? Was I stupid? Was I limited regarding the type of career I could have? Would I be able to keep this a secret from my family and friends? Mrs. Fehr told me to calm down and relax. Then she told me that I wasn't stupid. I just learned differently. She said I was one of the smartest people she had ever met. She said I could be an astronaut if I wanted to. She explained that dyslexia (pronounced dis-**lek**-see-uh) is a learning problem some people have with reading and writing. It can make words look jumbled. This makes it difficult for a person to read and remember what was read. "So what's going on inside my brain?" I asked her. She told me it didn't mean I was dumb. In fact, many very smart people have dyslexia. "How smart?" I asked. "Well," she said, "some people say Albert Einstein was dyslexic." The problem does occur in the brain, though. Sometimes the messages the brain is sending get jumbled up or confused. A person who has dyslexia might get frustrated and find it hard to do schoolwork. But the good news was that dyslexia doesn't have to keep a person down. Just having a name for what I had been battling in my head my whole life was an upper for me. And you can imagine how good it felt to learn from Mrs. Fehr that I was entitled to modifications in the classroom and while taking exams.

Dyslexic people are visual, multi-dimensional thinkers. I am intuitive and highly creative, and I excel at hands-on learning. Because I think in pictures, it is sometimes hard for me to understand letters, numbers, symbols, and written words. But, I can learn to read, write, and study, and my test scores more accurately reflect my knowledge when I use methods geared to my unique learning style.

One day in Mrs. Fehr's office, I sat and daydreamed about when I was a little boy and I looked at the events in my life up until that moment. It all began to make sense. I had always taken too long to do my work. I skipped, repeated, or omitted words when reading aloud. I had difficulty sounding out words and I consistently misspelled them. Also, I had poor reading comprehension and following instructions was difficult for me. I always had difficulty taking notes and I reversed letters like *b* and *d* and words like *was* and *saw*. I struggled with fill-in-the-blank answers, avoided writing assignments, and had a hard time getting my work done in the allotted time. Not to mention the hours I spent doing my homework and the frustration I felt with those adults who were always encouraging me to work up to my abilities. I remembered how in elementary and middle school I was sent to the "slow class," but I never stayed more than a few days before I was moved back into my regular classes. I never understood why. Sometimes people made fun of me because I had horribly mispronounced a word because in my mind that's the way the word sounded, and deep down inside I would feel like an idiot.

How in the world did I graduate from high school with advanced placement honors? Mrs. Fehr said it was sheer determination. At an early age I had innately taught myself, doing the best I could with the knowledge I had. When I started to advance in school and the material became more difficult, I forced myself to work harder. In my college classes I was color coding my notes way before I learned it was a tool used by people with dyslexia for taking better notes.

One afternoon as Mrs. Fehr and I talked, I recalled watching an episode from *The Cosby Show* in which Theo came home from school and told his parents he was dyslexic. Upon hearing that, Theo's siblings gave their dad a hard time, telling him that after all the years he had stayed on top of Theo about his studying and grades, it wasn't even his fault because he had been dyslexic his whole life. Wow! I could relate. Even though it was a huge relief to find out that I was dyslexic, almost a year went by before I was ready to tell my parents. My mom had the usual mom-type of inspiring response: "Keep doing your best and somehow everything will be alright." My dad's response was a little rougher around the edges, but it was just as important as the one I got from my mom. Dad had come to visit me at HSU, as he often did, and I remember telling him about my dyslexia in the parking lot of a Wal-Mart. I was very hard to tell him because I was afraid of looking weak in his eyes. His comments were more point-blank than my mom's: "It's not the end of the world," he said. "So what. Just deal with it. You know what you have and what you need to do, so just keep pushing forward." In a sense, I needed that response. I didn't like the way it sounded at first, but now, as I look back, I know it gave me that jolt I needed to get my life in gear.

Mrs. Fehr shared with me the names of famous people who were dyslexic: Tom Cruise, Cher, Walt Disney, Thomas Edison, General George Patton, Nelson Rockefeller, Pablo Picasso, Leonardo da Vinci, Richard Branson, Sir Winston Churchill, John F. Kennedy, and Muhammad Ali, and the list went on and on. She went a step further and told me about one of her friends, Dr. Charles Bloomer, who was an oral and maxillofacial surgeon. He was also a pilot, and he was dyslexic. She gave me his phone number and I set up a time to go by his office and meet him. Dr. Bloomer was truly gifted. We befriended one another and I began to shadow him on Thursdays, an activity that continued until I graduated.

During my college years I lived under the misconception that being popular or cool meant acting as if everything in my life was perfect. Perfect did not include a learning disability. I have since learned that disabilities are not bad, and being popular for me no longer means everything in my life is perfect. In fact, it is more important that it's not! Thinking of myself as imperfect doesn't mean I won't be successful. I may even be the person someone looks up to some day and then decides if Jonathan can be vulnerable and embrace his learning disability, why can't I. I didn't look at it that way in the beginning. It has taken me several years to adopt this new attitude. At first, all I could think was that I was all alone and less than. Nothing could have been further from the truth. The hardest part for me was surrendering and taking the first step towards getting help—a lesson I was to learn again years later concerning my sex addiction.

The next big step for me on the path to medical school was to take the Medical College Admission Test, commonly know as the MCAT. I was in foreign territory. Every time I thought I was getting ahead of the game, I found myself a few plays behind. I was not aware that people normally applied to medical school a year in advance. When I took the MCAT, it was given twice a year, once in April and again in August. Let's say you took the test in April and got a bad score. You could retake it in August. Actually you could take it as many times as you wanted (at one hundred and eighty-five dollars a pop!). MCAT scores ranged from a possible three to forty-five. Normally, a person scored between twenty-five and thirty-five. When applying to med school, a person with a low GPA could increase her chances of being accepted with a really good score on the MCAT. On the other hand, if a person had a really high GPA, but scored a twenty on the MCAT, this could really hinder his chances of being accepted. The MCAT score was not the only consideration for admission to medical school. Volunteering, shadowing, your personal statement, and extracurricular activities all played an important role in determining a person's acceptance. But a horrible score on the MCAT would ruin your chances for admission.

My first opportunity to take the MCAT, April of 2002, had passed. My next chance to take the exam was in August. Before taking the exam, it was recommended that I take some sort of prep course to prepare for the exam. I signed up for the Kaplan MCAT Review which cost about fourteen hundred dollars and was considered the best prep course on the market. Each section of the exam—verbal reasoning, physical sciences, writing sample, and biological sciences—was broken down and covered extensively by people who had taken the exam and scored extremely well in those sections. I was given full access to any resource I could possibly need to prepare for the exam. Plus, I could take as many practice exams as I could handle before I took the big one. My dad, who always broke the bank to support me with whatever journey I was on, gave me the money for the course. The only problem was, the closest location where the course was being offered was the University of Texas at Arlington, over one hundred and seventy miles away. Will Smith once said, "The road to success is through commitment and through the strength to drive through that commitment when it gets hard." And that was the attitude I adopted to motivate myself on my "road" to the MCAT.

One of my close friends, Matt Hamilton (I called him Bonner), was in a similar situation. He was also applying to medical school and always seemed to be a few steps behind. We both wanted to take the exam and apply to med school before the October deadline. We both were applying later than normal, but still shooting to get an interview between November and January.

It has often been said that when you are doing things according to God's plan, everything just seems to fall into place. Timing is perfect and everything just flows. Unfortunately, I seemed to be moving in the opposite direction of whatever God had planned for me and for the next two years I never felt so rushed in my life. Bonner and I quickly became road dogs, making the drive together from HSU to UTA on Mondays and Wednesdays. We would leave Abilene around 12:30 p.m., make it to Arlington around 3:00 p.m., study at the center until 5:30, grab a bite to eat, go to the review session from 6:00-9:00 p.m., and drive back to Abilene. I was also enrolled in summer school, shadowing doctors, and working three nights a week. Applying to medical school was one of the most frustrating experiences of my life because the more I thought I knew, the less I realized I actually knew. As the exam grew nearer, Bonner and I were taking practice exams on Saturdays and traveling to UTA three times a week.

The scores I was making on practice exams were sixes, sevens, and, every once in a while, a fourteen or a sixteen. Overall, they were absolutely horrible. As with all my other exams, I just kept on smiling. My life at that time could have been the lyrics of a country western song: "The handwriting on the wall was tellin' me to face the music, but the pride in my heart was tellin' me to just keep on pushing." Finally that day in August arrived. I had asked for and received all the modifications that a person with dyslexia could have when taking the MCAT; including a private room and extra time and a half. I took the test and then I waited. It took about a month and a half to receive my score in the mail, and as I waited I continued to apply to all of the medical schools in Texas.

It was while I was filling out those applications, in particular, while I was working on the personal statement section of the applications, that I began to question if I really had a true desire to become a doctor. The personal statement section was a very important opportunity to sincerely express my reasons for wanting to become a doctor. For many other applicants there had been magical, inspiring experiences while volunteering, or being a physician was a family tradition. Mrs. Fehr helped me with grammatical errors so that my statement would flow, but for me becoming a doctor was a materialistic goal, never a dream. My dream was to be a motivational speaker.

My reasons for wanting to be a doctor were all superficial— money, prestige and ego satisfaction. I felt that if I made a lot of money then I could afford to take a risk and pursue my real dream, and I would have the credentials of being a doctor to make me look good. Now, I couldn't exactly write that in my personal statement, so I struggled with my statement and never did get past the superficial reasons. I hoped that I would be able to arrange interviews based on all of my volunteer work and then I would talk my way into medical school.

I sent applications off to all the medical schools in the state and waited for my MCAT score. Other than Saran, I have never told anyone the actual score I made on the MCAT. It was a nine! Just writing that has helped lift a heavy burden I had placed on my shoulders. I don't know if it was the lowest score in the history of the exam, but that's what it was, a nine. If I was unable to meet the average requirements, how could I expect anyone to listen to what I had to say about what I would bring to their medical school if was accepted?

Soon after I got my MCAT score, I began to receive rejection letters; eventually, one from every med school I had applied to. And then I began to get a lot more mail from medical schools in the Caribbean islands. In the spring of 2003, my last semester at HSU, I got an enrollment package from St. Martinus University, which is a small medical school in Curacao-Dutch Antilles, an island located next to the island of Aruba and not too far off the coast of Venezuela. So I applied and I was accepted! Of course, my conscience was telling me there was something very odd about me getting accepted, considering my MCAT score. Not to mention that my GPA was below a 3.0. The school required that I retake the MCAT and the pre-med course I had taken at HSU, but this was a fairly new medical school so getting accepted was definitely better than the alternative. Deep down, and in spite of my acceptance to St. Martinus, my true feelings were telling me that this was not the best route for me to go. But I was still not ready to face the music. I was full of pride and determined to get into medical school.

I continued to impersonate the perfect life and on graduation day I had it in high performance: my family was there to celebrate with me, I was dating a beautiful local news anchor at the time, and I had a promising future with my acceptance to St. Martinus University Medical School.

Shortly thereafter, though, I finally took a closer look at exactly what attending St. Martinus would involve, and, truthfully, it didn't seem feasible. The main problem was, at that time, St. Martinus did not have a federal school code which meant I was unable to obtain financial aid. School started August 5 and it was going to cost me about $14,000 just for the first semester! That did include tuition and dorm fees, but it didn't include a laptop, books, an airplane ticket, and other supplies. Altogether, I was looking at a cost of about twenty grand and I only had a thousand.

John Lennon once said, "Life is what happens while you're making plans." That certainly was true for my life. I began to feel like my back was against the wall again, because I didn't have enough money. I had moved back to Houston where I could stay with my dad and save some rent money until it was time to leave for the islands. I decided the next thing to do was ask for help. The church where I had been a junior deacon and a member for my entire life, gave me a thousand dollars to help with my first semester. My stepmom, bless her heart, wrote a heartfelt letter to Oprah Winfrey asking for her help, and for about a month, I emailed Oprah almost every day. I even wrote to Magic Johnson.

During the previous summer I had attended a friend's wedding and during the reception I met a highly motivated man named Roger. He appeared to have the type of lifestyle I was hoping to enjoy by becoming a doctor. In fact, Roger was hosting the reception and it was lavish. I talked with him throughout the reception, telling him everything about my life and all of my hopes and dreams. Roger wished me all the best with my goals and with my life, and was kind enough to share some of his wisdom with me. We kept in touch over the months to come.

While the deadline for enrolling in St. Martinus drew near, I explained my situation to Roger and he offered to pay half of my first semester costs if I could come up with the other half. A man that I had met only once wanted to give me ten thousand dollars for medical school! I will always be thankful for Roger's generous offer and his willingness to help.

Up to that point, I had been so determined to attend St. Martinus that I had closed my mind to any other ideas or options regarding a "Plan B." But, as I considered Roger's offer, it occurred to me that even if I had the money to attend the first semester, when it was time for the second semester to begin, I would run into the same problems all over again. Finally, after a long talk with one of my mentors, Dr. Brock, I decided against attending St. Martinus University.

Now it was time for a Plan B: get a job in the medical field, save my money, retake the MCAT, and reapply to med school. August 5 came and went while I was spending my days at Houston's Medical Center trying to get a job in the medical field. Becoming a doctor had become such a part of who I thought I was, I had become afraid to do anything else. After looking for a job for about a month all over the Houston area and almost completely running out of graduation money, my fears diminished with the realization that I needed a job, fast. So I applied at the Pappadeaux Seafood Kitchen restaurant and started waiting tables again.

I signed up for the Kaplan MCAT Review in January of 2004 and this time I paid for the Kaplan Review myself. I was preparing to retake the exam in April. But, honestly, by this time

I was just going through the motions. I went to all the review sessions and took all of the practice exams but, simply put, I didn't have the passion to continue on. I did take the exam in April and this time my score improved a little—I scored an eleven!

T. S. Elliot said, "I've only to try, the rest is not my business." I had reached a low point in my life. I was not going to take the MCAT a third time in August. I knew that it wasn't going to do me any good to apply to any medical schools. I was feeling lousy and I was watching porn and randomly sleeping with women for comfort. Because I didn't get my MCAT results until late July, from April till July I lived a lie—pretending I had everything under control. I began to feel a distance between myself and God. The more I pressed myself to keep up the masquerade, the further away I felt from God.

Everyone in my world was convinced that I was going to be a sports orthopedic surgeon but me. During that summer I was in a new relationship with an amazing young doctor who was doing her residency at Baylor College School of Medicine. She had a neighbor named DaRhonda who I had met in passing while I was over at my girlfriend's place. Over the next few weeks I would see DaRhonda off and on at my girlfriend's and on this one occasion, DaRhonda asked me if I would like to grab a bite to eat with her one evening. At the time, I thought her invitation was sort of odd considering DaRhonda was married and I was dating her friend, but neither woman seemed to make a big deal out of it so I said ok. A few days later, while I was eating with DaRhonda on the patio of this little café, she looked me right in the eye and said, "You don't really want to become a doctor, do you, Jonathan." I didn't know how to respond. She continued on and asked me what it was that I was running from. I began to do my little bob and weave. *I could become an orthopedic surgeon. I have the ability, talent, and intelligence.* But I just didn't have the energy to defend myself. In my mind I heard the words of Bob Huggins (who at the time was the head basketball coach at the University of Cincinnati), "If you don't have any passion for what you are doing, then why do it." Friend, that is the difference between a job and a hobby that happens to be a job...passion. While talking with DaRhonda, I felt like I was back in Dr. Landwer's office. Except this time I was waiting to be told what I *really* had the ability to accomplish with my life. I had known what I wanted to do since I was a young boy, but I was scared because I didn't have all the answers. I was scared because I didn't know in what direction to start. I was scared because I was going to have to surrender my life completely over to God and give Him control. I was going to have to make some lifestyle changes. Finally, I just took a deep breath and said, "I want to be a motivational speaker. I want to inspire people, serve them, and ease their pain and suffering."

It felt like a ton of bricks had fallen off my shoulders once I began sharing with DaRhonda. She told me that she was a personal life coach. DaRhonda also had a special gift—one that reminded me of the stories my great-grandmother had shared with me about people whose hearing was just a little bit better than the average person's. Not trying to sound like a weirdo, but DaRhonda had the God-given ability to hear the whisper of God.

I had accepted Christ in my life as my Lord and Savior when I was around eight years old and I had been going to church all of my life. Whenever I had a transition in my life that caused me to move to another city, I would always search out and visit different churches until I found one where I could continue to grow spiritually. I also read my Bible and meditated daily. But deep down I felt that God only loved me if I was doing "the right things." I felt that if I made a mistake, God would punish me. If

I was good, God would have to be good to me. While sitting on the patio with DaRhonda, I began to surrender my life over to God and to the will of God. God's timing is always right on time—I had heard those words my whole life and when I met DaRhonda, I knew they were Truth with a capital T.

DaRhonda told me that she knew this wasn't the first time someone had told me about my God-given gift and how I was supposed to share it with the world. She knew she didn't have to tell me what I should do because I already knew. She said to me that she knew my Bear Mama and Big Mama had both prophesized my future to me when I was young. She took my breath away because only a handful of people knew what my grandmother and great-grandmother had shared with me and DaRhonda was not one of them. I knew what she was telling me was real. She told me that I needed to step into living my dream and become a speaker. She shared with me that I had the gift to communicate with the human spirit and to fill places with thousands of people who would come to hear me speak. I'm so grateful and honored to have met DaRhonda. After our talk, I knew it was time for me to stop running from myself and my destiny. People have often asked me why didn't I become a doctor and I tell them that being a doctor wasn't God's plan for me. I was playing the correct sport, just the wrong position.

I knew that if I was going to begin to make some lifestyle changes, the first one was to climb out of the dark pit I had dug for myself called sex addiction. By admitting I was a sex addict, I realized I was suffering from much more than a bad habit I could control if I just worked a little harder. I had become powerless to my sex addiction and my life was unmanageable. I was obsessed with sex; I acted out through compulsive masturbation, internet porn, pornographic magazines and videos, adult video stores, and relationships based on sex. I lied to myself and others. I had reached a point where I knew that I was fighting with my addiction and I felt my reality was altered. Dick Morris, President Bill Clinton's political advisor, described it best when during an interview with a Washington newspaper, he acknowledged that he had been egotistical and out of control before his precipitous fall from grace. He ignored his wife, he ignored his friends, and he ignored the rules.

"My sense of reality was altered," Morris told the Associated Press. "I started out being excited working for the president. Then I became arrogant; then I became grandiose and then I became self-destructive." His hands shook and his voice quivered as he struggled for the words to explain what led him to a year-long tryst with a call-girl and a lengthy relationship with another woman which included the birth of a child, all the while married to his wife Eileen. Both relationships were revealed in tabloids during the presidential campaign. And then Morris said these words: "It's too simple to say it was a sexual addiction. Saying I was sick, like I had pneumonia or the mumps—it's not that at all. I had—*no, I have* a fundamental flaw in my character, a fundamental weakness in my personality, a fundamental sin, if you will. I'm prone to believing that the rules don't apply to me." I too was out of touch with who I really was. But above all, I was ready to give that all up and get help.

During the summer of 2004, I had been trying to fill a void in my life with sex. I was surrounded by family and friends but inside I felt very lonely. If I had a good day, I needed sex to make it just a little better; porn, compulsive masturbation, or friends with benefits. The same went for a bad day—I would need some form of sex to feel better. I needed sex to help me release my frustrations and relax. I was no longer living in the present or in reality. I was constantly searching for the next great orgasm to make it all better. I believed the greater the sex, the stronger the love. I believed that love was something I could control.

I didn't get a divorce, lose my job, or contract a sexually transmitted disease as a result of my addiction. Actually, I felt that what was happening to me was much worse. Every time I acted out, I experienced a disconnection from God that was more defeating to me than anything else in the world. It didn't matter how often I went to church. It felt like the spiritual connection I had with God was dying. Then one day, while on the computer looking at porno websites, I noticed a little icon flashing in the corner of the screen. I clicked on it. It took me to a webpage that addressed sex addiction. I began to read and answer in my head some questions I found there which were designed to help the reader determine if he or she was a sex addict. I answered yes to 13 out of 15. Even as I was answering the questions, I continued to click back and forth between them and the porn. That is how lost I was, and I knew I needed help. I was at my lowest point spiritually. I was in my pit of hell.

Yet, despite all that, eventually I began to know that God was there, standing right there beside me, loving me and waiting for me. You cannot tell me that God Almighty will not go to the depths of the earth to get one of His lost sheep. I know He will because He did it for me. I know your Higher Power will do it for you. I had never felt so peaceful about my life as I did after I walked into my first sex addicts anonymous meeting and saw I wasn't the only person battling with sex addiction, and that there was actually a name for it. I honestly feel that sex addiction is an epidemic in the world today that is only dealt with in whispers. In October of 2004, I started attending a twelve-step program, got a sponsor, and have been in recovery ever since. Paul Valery said, "Every beginning is a consequence—every beginning ends something." Recovery is a beginning, a rebirth, the dawn of a new life. It is not simply a miracle which comes from heaven. It is the effect of my desire to change, to create my life anew with the help of God. Recovery is also an ending, the ending of old ways of behaving. I needed to mourn the passing of my old self, because my old self and I had become very close during all those years. At times I do miss my addiction, and I have to acknowledge that. But with patience I have learned to find new goals for my energies and new aims for my desires. What has ended is a way of life that led me into pain, sorrow, and hopelessness. I can let go now, for it is over and I am on the path of new beginnings.

As I stated in chapter one, I was baptized when I was eight; however, I did not get saved until I was twenty-three. I had accepted God in my life as my Lord and Savior when I was baptized but I was still lost. My mother didn't know me, my father didn't know me, my brothers didn't know me, my grandparents didn't know me, my girlfriends didn't know me...I didn't even know me. But God knew me. He knew me and He saved me. God knew what I had done. He knew my strengths and my weakness. He knew my fears and my addiction. He knew what I was running from and what I was running to. He knew my potential and what I was to become. He knew me completely and He saved me.

It's been said, "If you're not allowed to fail then how can you succeed?" As I started in this *New Direction* with my life, my grandmother told me one morning over breakfast how gold gets its awesome shine. She said, "Do you know how gold gets that pretty shine, that finished look? It is sent through fire. God is sending you through fire so that He can harden you and then turn you into polished gold." Simply put: Preparation. You can't have a testimonial unless you have been through trials and tribulations. Becoming a doctor is what I wanted, but becoming a doctor was too small for what God wanted me to become. I needed to travel this path in life to develop into the person God wanted me to be.

A friend of mine, Kim Wood, often says, "Every day you wake up you either make a decision that is going to get you a step closer to achieving your goal or cause you to take a step back from accomplishing your goal." What steps are you taking today to lead yourself in the right direction?

Chapter 6
The Truth Lies in Me

"And I am convinced and sure of this very thing, that He who began a good work in you will continue until the day of Jesus Christ [right up to the time of His return], developing [that good work] and perfecting and bringing it to full completion in you."
-Philippians 1:6 (AMP)

I was born into this world blessed with a special gift of being able to genuinely touch and communicate with the human spirit. I have always been able to walk into a room or any other setting and connect with people I have never seen before in my life. Where most people are fearful of public speaking, I am completely at peace. I feel a spiritual connection in my soul whether I am speaking with 2 people or 200 people. I feel like I am a vessel just opening my mouth and letting out what was placed on my heart to share with the world.

But for most of my life I used my God-given gifts and talents for my own self-manifestation. In Matthew, chapter 15, Jesus explains to the disciples what defiles a man after the Pharisees tried to entrap Jesus concerning the traditions of the elders. In verses 18 and 19, Jesus says, "But those things which proceed out of the mouth come forth from the heart; and they defile a man. For out of the heart proceed evil thoughts, murders, adulteries, fornications, thefts, false witness, and blasphemies: These are the things which defile a man." Instead of sharing my authentic self with the world, I used my gifts and talents for personal gain. I knew just the right words to say to an attractive woman to convince her to have sex with me. Instead of trusting my inner knowing of what I was meant to do, I used my gifts and talents to pursue a career as a doctor for recognition and material gain.

President Ronald Regan was known as "the great communicator" and is often remembered for the words he quoted from the Bible: "A city on a hill cannot be hidden." I feel he made a powerful statement which helped inspire a nation. The verses he was referring to are Matthew 4:14-16, "You are the light of the world. A city on a hill cannot be hidden. Neither do people light a lamp and put it under a bowl. Instead they put it on its stand, and it gives light to everyone in the house. In the same way, let your light shine before men, that they may see your good deeds and praise your Father in heaven."

I want to let my light shine before men, especially before my family and friends, and at the same time I have thoughts in my head of failure and of being rejected by those same people after they read this book. There are some subjects covered in this book about which only a few people in my life know. I am afraid. I am afraid of success. I am afraid of doing the will of God. I am terrified of becoming a great motivational speaker, author, or, maybe one day, a pastor. I stand at a crossroad. I have a great life when I am sober. When I am acting out, I live scared. I am afraid that someone will ask me if I still struggle with sex addiction after they finish reading my book or during a speaking engagement or when I am counseling them. I don't want it to seem to the outside world that I don't have it together. I am afraid of answering, "Yes, I still struggle with sex addiction." When I choose not to write, exercise, or involve myself in the world, I am choosing to be a practicing sex addict. When I choose to trust in God and the will

He has for me and to take care of myself mentally, spiritually, and physically, I am choosing to be a recovering sex addict. When I act out, I am covering a shadow in my life that I do not want to look at. I am terrified of being successful, but I am more horrified of living life as a practicing sex addict.

When I spend too much time in my head, I become detached from living my life from my heart and trusting in a Higher Power—one greater than my own. Alan Catanese, a talented poet, wrote a poem entitled *Heart vs. Head* and in it he says:

"There is no doubt about it—my mind is a great gift. But I am equally aware that the three pounds of gray matter wobbling around on top of my neck can often be more of a problem than a solution. Because of its lofty perch, my head seems certain that it was meant to be in charge of my life. However, the truth is that my head spends much of its time manufacturing problems, fear and desires that are not real. Like a hamster in its exercise wheel, my mind will run and run, without ever getting anywhere in its repeated attempts to figure things out. Several floors below, my heart sits patiently biding its time, knowing that sooner or later my brain will have worked itself into a froth that results in confusion and paralysis. In those moments, my heart steps in and gently places the truth of the situation before my weary mind, a truth it has known all along. If only my head would have stopped jabbering long enough to ask. Because while my head wonders, my heart knows."

Who does it benefit living only with the thought that I alone control my own fate? Let me tell you, friend, I have learned that when I live with that type of mentality, I'm limiting myself to a narrow and limited vision. Henley wrote the prophetic words, "I am the master of my fate; I am the captain of my soul." Napoleon Hill, author of the action-packed *Think & Grow Rich,* suggested Henley should have informed us that we are the masters of our fate and the captains of our souls because we have the power to control our thoughts. But I would like to go a step further and say I acquired the power to control my thoughts only after I gave the control over to God, my Higher Power. I have opened my mind to unlimited possibilities. When I have tried to control my destiny using the force of my will, the results have not always been positive. Now, as I learn to trust in the will that God has for me, yes, I am fearful, but the satisfaction of knowing I can do all things through Christ Jesus who strengthens me, helps to ease my weary mind.

My vision includes the belief that we can all achieve endless possibilities once we realize that the truth lies in each and every one of us. Marianne Williamson speaks to this idea so powerfully in her book *A Return to Love*:

"Our deepest fear is not that we are inadequate. Our deepest fear is that we are powerful beyond measure. It is our light, not our darkness, that most frightens us. We ask ourselves, who am I to be brilliant, gorgeous, talented, fabulous? Actually, who are you NOT to be? You are a child of God. Your playing small does not serve the world. There is nothing enlightening about shrinking so that other people won't feel unsure around you. We were born to make manifest the glory of God that is within us. It is not just in some of us; it is in everyone. As we let our own light shine, we unconsciously give other people permission to do the same. As we are liberated from our own fear, our presence automatically liberates others."

Wow! I often read those words when I feel myself losing sight of the big picture.

Yes, it's true, I am a *recovering* sex addict, and I stress the word "recovering." Addiction is a stunting illness that interferes with the healthy, forward movement of life. Sex addiction is not a glamorous affair. There is nothing intimate about it. It is scary, grimy, and lonely. I have actually heard people say they think they would like to be a sex addict, that it sounds like it would be so cool and fun. Anyone who says that is completely naïve or ignorant. For me, sex addiction is a spiritual disease. While I was living as a practicing addict, I was stripped from my spirituality. As a result, I was completely numb.

I can't lie. There is a love/hate relationship with the addiction. The hate is in the struggle. Sometimes this struggle can be handled as easily as turning to another channel or looking the other way. At other times it is more difficult, such as when I have to make myself get out of bed because I know that I am home alone for the morning and have constant access to the internet which is a major temptation. I can never forget that I am just a decision away from acting out. Will Garcia said, "The first step toward change is acceptance. Once you accept yourself, you open the door to change. That's all you have to do. Change is not something you do, it's something you allow."

The love is in my recovery. I was once told by a friend who is also a recovering sex addict something I found to be very insightful: recovery is the freedom to live in the truth. The truth is I can't experience the recovery of my addiction through my Higher Power without first knowing what it feels like to experience the hell of being self-absorbed in my addiction. I can't share with you how the sweetness of life tastes without truly tasting the bitter. I can't fully love Jonathan without first knowing what it feels like to hate Jonathan. Sidney J. Harris said, "It's surprising how many persons go through life without ever recognizing that their feelings toward other people are largely determined by their feelings toward themselves, and if you're not comfortable within yourself, you can't be comfortable with others." I must learn how to be my own best friend. Rob Bremer said, "If you had a friend who talked to you like you sometimes

109

talk to yourself, would you continue to hang around with that person?" There is freedom in being able to look yourself in the eye despite your imperfections. Elizabeth J. Canham wrote, "There is no freedom like seeing myself as I am and not losing heart." Miguel Ruiz said, "We have the need to be accepted and to be loved by others, but we cannot accept and love ourselves. The more self-love we have, the less we will experience self-abuse. Self-abuse comes from self-reflection, and self-rejection comes from having an image of what it means to be perfect and never measuring up to that ideal. Our image of perfection is the reason we reject ourselves the way we are, and why we don't accept others the way they are." What all this boils down to some words of wisdom my mentor, Michael Taylor, often shares with me: "We must learn to love ourselves to wholeness. We are in the love-them-to-wholeness business." And Buddha said long ago, "You, yourself, as much as anybody in the entire universe, deserve your love and affection."

I choose not to lose faith and I am constantly strengthened by working my program. I know that God is using me as a gift to be a blessing to my family, friends, and the world. I have learned that when I work at real problems and connect with people, I truly feel alive. For a good relationship to grow, I need to give and receive genuine affection. I may slip today or some day in the future; there are no promises of perfection. I do, however, choose to keep moving forward in faith and live one day at a time. I believe it was Nietzsche who said, "Do not lust, live. Live with passion. Do not live a planned orderly life, take chances. Even the failures that may result from taking chances could be used to enhance personal growth."

"Enhance personal growth" is an understatement. Recovery has allowed me to experience unimaginable new heights in my life, but I could not have recovery unless I had something to learn and recover from. Therein lies the love/hate relationship with my addiction. The Apostle Paul wrote in Romans 5:3-5, "Moreover let us exult and triumph in our troubles and rejoice in our sufferings, knowing that pressure and affliction and hardship produce patient and unswerving endurance. And endurance develops maturity of character. And character produces joyful and confident hope of eternal salvation. I can be spiritual and I don't have to be guilty anymore."

God has kissed my life by blessing me with Saran, a beautiful woman who is absolutely a gift to my life. I have learned that I cannot control love. To love is to let go. I also cannot control the people who love me; their love is a gift. The first time I met Saran, I was studying to take the MCAT for my second time and she was studying for her first time. We went on a couple of dates and spoke on the phone a few times. I was self-absorbed and I was acting out all the time. After a short while, she told me to never call her again. She felt that I was egotistical, very arrogant, and she no longer wanted to talk to me. She was right on all accounts.

Eight months passed and I bumped into Saran at a local café. During those eight months I had made some significant personal changes in my life. I had surrendered to the trust and will of God and I was involved in a twelve-step program and had a sponsor. I had that amazing talk with DaRhonda and had stopped running away from my destiny. I had started working on my first book. And I had come to the realization that the reason I was always in and out of different relationships had very little to do with the other person and quite a lot to do with me! I couldn't blame my relationship problems on the other person anymore. The night I met with Saran again, I made small talk and I asked her out to dinner and, to my surprise, she accepted. A couple of days later we went out to dinner and she stopped me in the middle of our conversation and asked, "Who are you? You are not the man I knew eight months ago." I shared with her that I had made some personal changes, but I had not noticed that I had changed all that much. She felt that I had changed and she liked it. That was May 16, 2005. While I wasn't paying much attention, the truth within me was beginning to transform my life. While I felt I was just spinning my wheels, the layers on the onion were being peeled away. And now the time was right for my relationship with Saran. Timing is a very important thing, but it's not my timing or the other person's timing—it's God's timing.

At the end of July, Saran moved to Dallas to begin medical school. From the beginning of our relationship I was honest and up front with her, and I told her that I was a recovering sex addict. To my amazement, she did not run away. While Saran was in medical school in Dallas, I was living in Houston. I was beginning my second year of management at a restaurant where I had been working since I had graduated from HSU. My track record for being faithful was 0 to a lot and with Saran living over three hours away, it was easy to see why some people may have had their doubts about our relationship. But, unlike the past, we both put our faith and trust in God and we made it. After living apart for nine months and only seeing each other every couple of weeks for a few days, I knew it was time for me to take a step outside of my comfort zone, to deepen my faith, and move a step closer towards my dreams.

In March of 2006, I read an awesome book written by Spencer Johnson, M.D., called *Who Moved My Cheese?* The book tells of an amazing way to deal with change in your work and in your life. I highly recommend it. Most people probably apply this book's wisdom to their current job situation, but I applied it to my life. I realized it was time for me to get serious about writing this book you are now reading and pursuing my dreams of being a motivational speaker. I also realized that since I had practically zero responsibilities to anyone other than myself, the time was right for me to make a move to Dallas.

As I prayed over everything, praying only for the knowledge of God's will for me and the power to carry it out, I knew I was making the right decision. I informed my restaurant's general manager and corporate office of my plans. I was open and honest with them and I let them know I was putting in my two weeks' notice so that I could move to Dallas to be with Saran, work less hours, and focus on finishing my book and becoming a dynamic motivational speaker. I was doubtful of their support and I was prepared to take a pay cut in order to find a job with less responsibilities. Eight managers before me had left the restaurant I was working at and their departures had been frowned upon.

The response I received was simply amazing! Not only did the corporate office support my decision, they also offered me a job as a waiter at their Dallas steakhouse—Pappas Brothers Steakhouse. To be a server at Pappas Brothers Steakhouse is an absolute honor. Not only would I be making more money but I would be working fewer hours than I had as a manager. The Steakhouse is considered the "Rolls Royce" of all the other Pappas concepts. Only the best of the best work at the Steakhouse. It is known for providing the highest quality of service and product. There is a waiting list just to get an interview. Corporate told me that this is how much they valued me. I happened to know one the managers of the Steakhouse in Houston and also the new regional manager in Houston who had recently moved there from Dallas, and they both knew the general manager of the Steakhouse in Dallas. They both spoke with him and put in a good word for me.

I flew to Dallas for an interview with the general manager and guess what…I actually had met him a year prior to the interview at a corporate meeting and I had made a lasting, good impression on him. When I walked into the restaurant he didn't exactly remember my name, but more importantly, he remembered my positive attitude and smile. We talked about everything, well, I mean I did most of the talking, about Saran, my goals, and my plan of action to reach my goals. I got the job.

Everything I needed to get the job had already been taken care of by God a year earlier. All I had to do was show up and introduce myself. From day one, Rick Turner, my general manager, made it perfectly clear that he was supportive of everything I wished to accomplish. And in addition to his support, I had the support of the other managers and staff. What a stress reliever. Not only did God bless me but He triple-blessed me: moving to Dallas to be with Saran, living my dreams of becoming a best-selling author and motivational speaker, and working at Pappas Brothers Steakhouse. (By the way, an article in the December 2007 issue of *Texas Monthly* recognized Pappas Brothers Steakhouse as the best steakhouse in Texas. One could argue that it is the best in the country!)

After moving to Dallas, I joined an organization called Toastmasters. Toastmasters is an international organization which helps people face their fear of public speaking, improve their speaking gifts to become outstanding speakers, and maximize their leadership skills. The chapter I joined was known as Exceed Toastmasters and with the help of my fellow Toastmasters, after presenting the ten required speeches, I have achieved competent communicator status. Friend, you can't tell me God isn't good when you begin stepping out on faith and know that the truth lies within you!

I have always been a dreamer and so I loved reading (former Toastmaster) Napoleon Hill's classic *Think & Grow Rich*. He wrote, "If the thing you wish to do is right and you believe in it, go ahead and do it! Put your dream across, and never mind what 'they' say if you meet temporary defeat, for 'they,' perhaps, do not know that every failure brings with it the seed of an equivalent success." I wanted to be a doctor, a husband, and an entrepreneur, all through sheer determination and not because I wanted to, but because I thought I needed to in order to gain wealth and fame. I was sacrificing sincere happiness by trying to put myself into a life I thought was golden, while not trusting that the real riches in life come from inside the soul by living a life of authenticity.

Most of the time I am able to regard being dyslexic as an awesome gift. But sometimes I forget what a blessing it is especially when I have to study longer or read an article two or three times before it clicks in my brain. The good news is that most of the time when whatever it is that I am struggling to learn finally does click in, I have no doubt that I am going to remember it forever. Also, people with dyslexia are extremely intelligent. I am a visual learner and being dyslexic helps me mentally recall experiences I have gone through in life and then I can paint with words a clear picture for the people with whom I am sharing.

I know what it takes to be a champion on the football field. While at Hardin-Simmons, I had the honor of playing for the state's "winningest" college football team during one-fourth of its sixteen-year winning streak. I have four championship rings to prove it. But even better than all that external evidence, I now believe in my God-given abilities and I know that I am a champion playing in the game of life. Everyday I wake up and I step onto that playing field called the real world and I play the greatest game of my life. My teammates are the people that God brings into the game so I can encourage them to believe in their abilities, and in return they help me move closer to becoming the man God wants me to be. I love it!

I wasn't sure of the direction I needed to take to get involved with motivational speaking but, unlike when I decided I wanted to be a doctor, this time I simply prayed to God that I was going the right way. My church life started in Giddings and has moved with me to Abilene, Houston, and now Dallas. In every stage of my life I have been involved with a church and I have had close relationships with the pastors of those churches. As I moved from one church to the next, I gradually learned what I believe is most important—the church first begins *in* you and me. We must realize that the dreams we want to achieve in life must be born from feelings of joy and worthiness within ourselves, not from desires for outer material objects. If it felt like I was preaching, I apologize. I'm not an expert on religion; all I can do is share with you, friend, what I know, and I know I have come a long way and it is all because of the goodness of my Higher Power. When I speak about God, I'm not concerned about what religion you are. You may be Christian, Jewish, Hindu, Muslim, or Buddhist. Your belief is your choice. I'll just keep it simple; my belief is that God is my Higher Power and to get to him I must go through His son Jesus Christ.

I didn't know it at the time, but when I thought I was running from who God wanted me to be, I was actually running right into His arms. He was developing me from within and molding me into the person I needed to become to do His will. He is not finished developing me though; my spiritual salvation is a process.

I am a work in progress. Earlier in this book, I spoke about never being faithful to anyone other than Saran. The truth is I have never been faithful to anyone, not to Saran, not even to myself. The fact that I have lusted after women—holding images in my mind as I fantasized and, self-absorbed in my addiction, clicking on screen after screen of pornographic images on my computer—is a form of being unfaithful. I am a work in progress. I also told you about my affirmation, "As a man among men, I am faithful and true." For many years, I thought that "as a man among men, I am faithful and true" meant I had to be perfect— that in order to be considered a success, my life had to be lived perfectly without mistakes, and because of that belief I experienced a lot of worry, self-doubt, shame and fear. Recently, as I reflected more on my affirmation, I began to see that I could accept my flaws and past mistakes and still be faithful and true. My affirmation now means that I am able to look myself in the eye and openly admit that I have made mistakes and I have used poor judgment. It means I can ask for forgiveness and, as scary as it may sound or as painful as it may be, I can make amends with people whenever possible.

It also means that I am transparent with Saran. **We are transparent with each other and we talk openly and honestly about our shortcomings. We have learned to trust that this way of communicating with each other will serve to draw us closer. And it has. I feel that Saran's love for me is an example of the love God has for everyone in the world. Saran loves me unconditionally. There aren't enough words for me to say to her, enough gifts for me to give her or enough ways for me to show her how much her love means to me. She has given me the greatest gift anyone can hope to experience in his lifetime—an opportunity to love and be loved in return. Day after day after day, I love Saran and she loves me in return.**

No matter how afraid I might be, I can accept the consequences of my actions. Yes, I am a flawed man who has acted many times from selfish motives. However, and more importantly, I am a man who diligently strives for integrity, accountability and honor. That is why even when I have wanted to beat myself up with shame, I can look at myself in the mirror and I can gaze into Saran's beautiful, brown eyes. Being a faithful and true man is not easy; it takes a lot of courage. But, no matter what, at the end of the day I am a better man for it. The book of Proverbs says that God's people are like the dawning of the morning. We grow brighter and brighter until the day is full. The Apostle Paul said that he was not perfect, but he was pressing toward the mark day by day.

There will be times in your life where the truth that lies in you, just like in me, will become unclear and you may begin to want to give up and quit. Don't! You must hop on your bike and continue to pedal. Here are two poems that I must share with you that have helped me persevere when times were tough.

DON'T QUIT

When things go wrong, as they sometimes will,
When the road you're trudging seems all uphill,
When the funds are low and the debts are high,
And you want to smile, but you have to sigh,
When care is pressing you down a bit,
Rest, if you must, but don't you quit.

Life is queer with its twist and turns,
As every one of us sometimes learns.
And many a fellow turns about,
When he might have won had he stuck it out.
Don't give up, though the pace is slow.
You may succeed with another blow.

Often the struggler has given up
When he might have captured the victor's cup.
And he learned too late, when the night came down.
How close he was to the golden crown.
Success is failure turned inside out.
The silver tint in the clouds of doubt.
And you can never tell how close you are.
It may be near when it seems afar.
So stick to the fight when you're hardest hit.
It's when things seem worst that you must not quit.
Author Unknown

THE ROAD OF LIFE

At first, I saw God as my observer, my judge, keeping track of the things I
did wrong, so as to know whether I merited Heaven or Hell when I die. He
was out there sort of like the president, I recognized His picture when I
saw it, but I didn't really know Him.

But later when I recognized Him, it seemed as though life was rather like a
bike ride, but it was a tandem bike, and I noticed that God was in the back helping
me pedal.

I don't know just when it was that He suggested we change places, but life has
not been the same since. Life with Him, that is. God makes life exciting! When
I had control, I knew the way. It was rather boring, but predictable. It was the
shortest distance between two points.

But when He took the lead, He knew delightful long cuts, up mountains, and
through rocky places at breakneck speeds; it was all I could do to hang on!
Even though it looked like madness, he said, "Pedal!"

I worried and was anxious and asked, "Where are you taking me?" He laughed and didn't answer, and I started to learn to trust.

I forgot my boring life and entered into the adventure. And when I'd say, "I'm
scared," He'd lean back and touch my hand.

He took me to people with gifts that I needed, gifts of healing, acceptance, and
joy. They gave me their gifts to take on my journey, our journey, God's and
mine.

And we were off again. He said, "Give the gifts away; they're extra baggage, too
much weight." So I did, to the people we met, and I found that in giving I
received, and still our burden was light.

I did not trust Him at first, in control of my life. I thought He'd
wreck it. But
He knows bike secrets, knows how to make it bend and take
sharp corners,
knows how to jump to clear high rocks, knows how to fly to
shorten scary passages.

And I am learning to shut up and pedal in the strangest places,
and I'm
beginning to enjoy the view and the cool breeze on my face with
my delightful,
constant companion, my Higher Power.

And when I'm sure I just can't do anymore, He just smiles and
says, "Pedal."
Author Unknown

Wow! Please keep these two poems close by so when you feel
down and out, you can read them. Whether taped on a wall, in a
frame on your desk, or in your pocket, refer to them often until
you can recall them by belief!

I wrote in Chapter 5 that I once felt all alone even though I had
family and friends in my life. I now agree with the words of
Apostle Paul in Romans, chapter 8, verses 38 and 39: "For I am
convinced that neither death nor life, neither angels nor demons,
neither the present nor the future, nor any powers, neither height
nor depth, nor anything else in all creation, will be able to
separate us from the love of God that is in Christ Jesus our Lord."

After everything I had experienced, from the discovery of my
dyslexia to the shadows of my sex addiction, and in spite of my
evolving spiritual relationship with God, there was one person

with whom I still needed to make amends—myself. I had come to a point in my life where I needed to redefine my image. Since 2001, DNA testing has freed twelve men in Dallas County court cases. The latest instance of DNA tests overturning old cases came this past January for fifty-year-old James Waller who had been convicted of raping a twelve-year-old boy in 1982—a crime he had always said he never committed. When asked how he felt about being wrongly convicted, Mr. Waller said, "I have no hatred towards anyone, because I have made my peace with God."

Each of us is constantly going through a metamorphosis and there will come a time in life when we must each redefine our image. Hopefully, it will not be at the magnitude James Waller experienced. No matter what the situation is, I do believe that there are three key factors in redefining an image: forgiveness, a positive attitude, and good deeds.

Forgiveness is the first key factor to redefining an image. Susan St. James said, "Having resentment is like taking poison and hoping the other person dies." Forgive the people that hurt you. Forgive that boss that did you wrong. Forgive that friend who betrayed you. Forgive that parent that mistreated you when you were younger. Get rid of all that poison. Don't let that root of bitterness grow deeper and continue to contaminate your life. What does this toxic waste look like in our lives? For some people it seeps out as anger. In others it looks like depression or it reeks of low self-esteem. We are not forgiving the people that hurt us for their sake, but for our sake. We are forgiving so we don't have to carry that baggage around anymore.

Over time it has become easier to forgive people who have harmed me or wronged me and move forward. Yet the person I find it hardest to forgive is me. I have asked God to forgive my sins, mistakes, and everything else in between and I know He has. So I asked myself: Am I above God? Do I expect more from myself than God does? If the answer to those two questions is no, then why do I insist on shaming and ridiculing Jonathan over past mistakes and wrong choices? My worst enemy, the person who holds me back, and the person I resent the most, is me. I know that I am not above God, that He wants more for me than I do for myself, that I am a child of God and He is my father, that He forgave David for his sins and David was a man made after God's own heart. Then who am I not to forgive Jonathan? I eventually wrote myself the following amends letter which has helped me to allow God to turn the key and free me from my self-made bondage:

Dear Jonathan Oliver,

I am sorry for making you feel so ashamed. I am sorry for not having more faith in you and for doubting you. I know that I have caused you a lot of pain and sadness in your life. I apologize for keeping you detached from reality because I had you confused and lost in fantasy. I regret not allowing you to be fully present and faithful in your past relationships. I am sorry for the physical pain and disgrace I have caused for your body. I am remorseful for the separation I believed there was between God and you. I am sorry for causing you to feel low self-esteem and feel unworthy of success. I regret the money I caused you to spend and the time you wasted on trying to make me happy. I am sorry for holding you back from being honestly present when you were with members of your family. I apologize for not allowing you to be focused on living your dreams by doing God's will with the gifts and talents He has so graciously blessed you. I apologize for making you feel so afraid and shameful about doing your best to please me instead of God.

I can't give back yesterday, Jonathan, and for that I am truly sorry. What I will give you from my heart is the love I have for you today and for the rest of my life. I love you, Jonathan Oliver. I sincerely love you.

Faithful and True,

Jonathan Oliver

After I finished writing the letter, I read it out loud, typed it and signed and dated it. Finally, I put it in a frame and placed it at the top of my bookcase beside my college degree. Since then I have truly felt the freedom of self-forgiveness and at those times when I feel that I am being too hard on myself or that there is no way my situation can improve, I read that letter I wrote to dear Jonathan Oliver.

Having a positive attitude is the next factor in redefining an image. Some examples of what you can do to have a positive attitude follow: Evaluate where you are. Ask yourself what brought you to this point. Are you learning new behaviors or are you merely doing the same thing over and over again? Doing the same thing over and over and continuing to get the same results is the definition of insanity. Stop and change your approach. Accept responsibility for your life—don't be a volunteer victim. Be determined to handle any challenge in a way that will make you grow.

Buddha said, "Holding on to anger is like grasping a hot coal with the intent of throwing it at someone else; you are the one getting burned." Take charge of your emotions. Learn to master them or they will master you. You see it almost every day in the newspapers or on your TV—someone is apologizing for letting their emotions get the best of them. Lastly, expect things to get better. Remember what Charles Swindoll said: "Life is 10% what happens to us and 90% how we react to it." Have a positive attitude.

Too much talk is just like chalk...you can rub it out. Napoleon Hill once said: "Deeds and not words are what count the most." Doing good deeds is the final factor in redefining an image. If you are spending a lot of time and energy feeling sorry for yourself, find someone you can help and forget about yourself for a while. Whenever I am having a self-pity day, I call my great-grandmother. She turned eighty-seven earlier this year and she is my "Big Mama." She enjoys a good conversation and she can talk for hours. Something special always happens during the course of our conversation. As we begin to say our good-byes to one another, I discover that whatever I was feeling down and out about is no longer as huge as I made it out to be. I suggest you give it a try the next time you're having a self-absorbed day—call a friend or relative and lose your troubles as you connect with a loved one. Hold a door open a few extra seconds and let some people in and out of a building. Slow down and let a few cars merge onto the freeway the next time you are in bumper-to-bumper traffic.

Three individuals who did not let their trials and tribulations stop them from going good deeds were Moses, Gandhi, and Nelson Mandela. Moses killed an Egyptian whom he saw beating a Hebrew slave. Fearing that he would have to answer to Pharaoh, Moses went into hiding for over forty years, until God spoke to him through a burning bush and we all know how the story ends. God used Moses to lead the Israelites out of Egypt where they had lived as slaves for over 400 years.

Gandhi had been imprisoned for many years on numerous occasions in both South Africa and India for his beliefs and practices. Throughout his life, Gandhi remained committed to non-violence and truth even in the most extreme situations which led India to independence and inspired movements around the world. In India he is recognized as the Father of the Nation. *Time* magazine named Gandhi "Man of the Year" in 1930 and runner-up to Albert Einstein as "Person of the Century" at the end of 1999. Gandhi never received the Nobel Peace Prize, though he was nominated for it five times between 1937 and 1948.

Nelson Mandela was in prison for twenty-seven years of his struggle against apartheid. Apartheid, meaning separatism, was a system of racial segregation that was enforced in South Africa beginning in 1948 and was finally dismantled in 1993. Nelson Mandela was the first president of South Africa to be elected in fully representative democratic elections. In 1993 he was awarded the Nobel Peace Prize for his work towards ending the apartheid regime and for laying the foundation for a new, democratic South Africa. According to *Time 100*, he is one of only four people in history to have shaped both the 20th and 21st centuries. The other three are Bill Gates, Pope John II, and Oprah Winfrey.

Performing good deeds was a key factor in the lives of Moses, Gandhi, and Nelson Mandela which allowed them to move forward through trials and tribulations and experience the true value of their lives.

Like James Waller, you free yourself from bondage when you forgive the people who hurt you. Have a positive attitude. Don't dwell on yesterday's disappointments or your past failures. Press forward and look for the goodness that is in store for you. When you are feeling sorry for yourself, do something nice for someone else. What you give is what you get. No matter what your situation is, I do believe forgiveness, a positive attitude, and good deeds are the key factors to redefining your image.

As I come full circle I feel like I am in a place like I first wrote about in Chapter 1, where God spoke to me and I joined the church at the very tender age of eight. Then, as I wrote in Chapter 5, fifteen years went by before I truly experienced being "saved." And now, after another five years, I find myself at a place where

I am consciously accepting God as being the Lord of my life. I am not a moment too late or a second too early. The feeling is the same I felt when I was eight; that pure feeling of simply loving God and allowing myself to experience God's love and grace. I am talking about praising Him, falling asleep praising Him and waking up praising Him. I feel like I have completed a journey to that place I once was in when I was a little boy.

Now I can see how, as I grew older and became more intellectual and "mature," I moved from my heart to running everything through my head. I unconsciously put God in the role of a parent. Neale Donald Walsch wrote in *Conversations with God*, "It is your parents who taught you that love is conditional—you have felt their conditions many times—and that is the experience you take into your own love relationships. It is also the experience you bring to me [God]." So, with God in a parental role, if I didn't do something a certain way or I did something wrong, then I would anger God and risk losing God's love. And I would worry about what I needed to do to keep His love.

As I have lived through the recovery of my addictions and experienced the freedom of my recovery, I have learned that God is God all by Himself and he doesn't need me for Him to be God. There is nothing I can do more or do less that is going to increase God's love for me or cause me to lose His love. God knows where, what time, the feelings I will have, and everything else I could ever imagine about every aspect of my life. My being a recovering sex addict has nothing to do with how much God loves me. He knew when He created me all my strengths and weaknesses, and they were all given to me to use in giving God all the praise and glory. There is nothing I have to do to earn God's love. His love is a gift. His grace is sufficient.

So I no longer need to waste energy fighting to keep God's love because it is there all the time. All I need to do is quiet my mind, listen, and enjoy the experience. The only prayer I need to pray to God is a simple prayer of gratitude. I need only to be thankful. This means I don't need to handcuff God and treat Him like my little genie. Walsch wrote in *Communion with God*, "Most people believe in God; they just don't believe in a God who believes *in them*. God does believe in them. And God loves them more than most of them know. The idea that God turned stone-silent and stopped talking to the human race a long time ago is false. The idea that God is angry with the human race and kicked it out of Paradise is false. The idea that God has set Himself up as judge and jury and will be deciding whether members of the human race go to heaven or go to hell is false. God loves every human being who ever lived, lives now, or ever will live. God's desire is for every soul to return to God, and God cannot fail in having this desire fulfilled. God is separate from nothing, and nothing is separate from God. There is nothing that God needs, because God is every thing there is. This is the good news. Everything else is an illusion."

Ralph Waldo Emerson said: "...to appreciate beauty; to find the best in others; to give one's self; to leave the world a little better, whether by a healthy child, a garden patch, or a redeemed social condition; to have played and laughed with enthusiasm, and sung with exultation; to know even one life has breathed easier because you have lived. This is to have succeeded."

I believe that my life is imperfectly perfect; there is no flawless way for me to live life. I have learned to just live life and live it to the fullest. True happiness for me comes from within.

...as I take a full, deep breath and exhale, I return to the present moment and gaze out my window with feelings of gratitude and hope—gratitude for the experiences I have had so far in my life which have helped shape me into the man I am, and hope for what the future holds as I continue on this journey.

CPSIA information can be obtained
at www.ICGtesting.com
Printed in the USA
FFOW03n1635050618
47024431-49322FF